Hugs Help

Our Story of Tragic Loss, Survival, and Helping Others

Randy Stocker

authorHOUSE®

AuthorHouse™
1663 Liberty Drive
Bloomington, IN 47403
www.authorhouse.com
Phone: 833-262-8899

Published by AuthorHouse 05/18/2022

ISBN: 978-1-6655-5937-9 (sc)
ISBN: 978-1-6655-5936-2 (hc)
ISBN: 978-1-6655-5935-5 (e)

Library of Congress Control Number: 2022908790

Print information available on the last page.

*Any people depicted in stock imagery provided by Getty Images are models,
and such images are being used for illustrative purposes only.
Certain stock imagery © Getty Images.*

This book is printed on acid-free paper.

*Because of the dynamic nature of the Internet, any web addresses or links contained in
this book may have changed since publication and may no longer be valid. The views
expressed in this work are solely those of the author and do not necessarily reflect the
views of the publisher, and the publisher hereby disclaims any responsibility for them.*

Contents

You can't sleep. It is 2:00 o'clock in the morning. You are crying so hard your body hurts. You can't eat. You can't feel anything. The sudden loss of your loved one, a child, a spouse, a sibling, a parent, has left you so emotionally drained you are uncertain if you can survive. You are not sure you want to survive. It. Just. Hurts. So. Much. The words and inaction of others have left you wondering if there is any humanity left in the world. I cannot fix it. There are no words to cure you.

I know. I have lived that scene for more than 18 years after losing my nineteen and nine-year old daughters and my mother through the careless actions of a truck driver.

Our story started on July 20, 2003, when our nineteen-year old daughter, Jenelle, told me that she wanted to visit my parents, her grandparents, in Gibson City, Illinois before going back for her second year of college at Drury University in Springfield, Missouri. Jenelle was planning to be an architect. Char, my wife, and I thought it was great that Jenelle wanted to spend more time with her grandparents. Not many teenagers take the time to make important visits like this. We were **SO PROUD OF HER**.

Did you ever make a good decision that turns out to be a terrible one? I did that day when I told Amy, our nine-year old, that she had to go with Jenelle to see my parents, Grandpa and Grandma Stocker. I have questioned my decision thousands of times and always come back to the same answer—it was the right thing to do.

They left on a Monday morning. Unfortunately, I was on a business call and was only able to wave goodbye to Jenelle and Amy. I sure wish that I had made the extra effort to give them a goodbye hug. They drove the three and one-half hours to Gibson City, Illinois and had a great evening with Dad and Mom. They watched movies, played games, and ate popcorn. Mom finished a blanket she was making for our son, Matt. He had not gone on the trip because he had football practice. Mom and Dad were so happy to be able to spend time with the girls.

The next day, Tuesday, July 22, Mom took the girls shopping in Bloomington, Illinois. They shopped at the mall, ate good food, and laughed all day long. Grandma spent a lot of money on the girls buying clothes for each girl for going back to school. Amy was going to be a fourth grader and was thrilled about going to a new school. Her new middle school had just told Amy that she would be in the TAG (Talented and Gifted) program. She was so excited to be part of TAG that she took the letter, cartwheeled, and did handstands around the neighborhood while telling everybody about this honor.

As they were leaving the mall in Bloomington, they called Char and told her how much fun they were having with Grandma Jean. They told her about where they ate and what Grandma had bought for each of the girls for their upcoming school years. It was a GREAT DAY as far as the girls were concerned.

Approximately fifteen minutes after talking to Char, our daughters were dead. They were driving back to Gibson City when a fully loaded, speeding semi-truck broadsided them. The driver was reading papers on the seat beside him at the time, missed the stop sign, and hit the car on the passenger side, right where Jenelle and Amy were sitting. From what we learned, Jenelle and Mom died instantly. We heard later from another driver that stopped to help that Amy was still alive and was making some sounds. He could not make out what she was saying. She died a few minutes later.

Our loss—Mom, Jenelle, and Amy
July 22, 2003

Our book is about the grief, pain, and suffering we went through that day and for years after that. We talk about our grieving, our marriage, and our suffering. We also talk about how we decided that we needed to help others with their grief. This book will concentrate mostly on grief caused by the sudden loss of life.

Approximately five months after the accident, someone we had never met before reached out to us for help. Her husband had been murdered. She needed to be with someone who was grieving as much as she was. By providing support to this woman and her family, we realized that helping others through their grief also helped us through ours.

This book will share with the reader the following:

1. How we suffered and what we did to "ease the pain" of suffering.
2. How we made sure that the memories of Jenelle, Amy, and Mom are remembered forever.

3. How we realized that helping others who were grieving became a calling for us.

4. How we came to understand that most people in our country do not know how to provide help, comfort, and assistance to grievers and most of the time do not even know what to do or say. We share several ideas of better ways to comfort those who are grieving. We learned that there are both helpful and hurtful things to do and say.

If you are struggling with his or her grief or someone who wants to help a friend or family member who is grieving, I believe this book will help. Below is our story.

The Nightmare Begins
It is 2:00 a.m; how do I survive?

Char and I were getting ready for dinner Tuesday, July 22, 2003, when we heard the doorbell ring. I looked out the front window and saw the sheriff's car. I had been receiving lots of fundraising calls from the local sheriff's department and figured somebody was here to make an in-person solicitation. I was not very happy with the interruption during dinnertime.

I opened the door and a person named Jim asked if he could speak to us. He encouraged us to sit down which I thought was a little rude. At that time, he asked, "Do you know Jean Stocker?" I said, "Of course I know her, she is my mom". He informed us that she died in a car wreck earlier in the day. At that time, Char and I began to panic because we knew that both Jenelle and Amy were with Grandma. Jim then told us that both Jenelle and Amy also died.

WOW! WOW! WOW! The thoughts that went through our minds at that time were things like:

"This must be a mistake." Char had just spoken to Jenelle and Amy a few hours earlier.

"He must have the wrong family. This kind of thing only happens to other people."

"God wouldn't let this happen to Mom, Jenelle, and Amy—they are good people and good Christians. Only bad people aren't protected by God."

Jim then asked me to call my dad, Frank Stocker. He and mom lived in Gibson City, IL. Dad's sister, Mary Lou, answered the phone and immediately handed it to Dad. All I could hear from Dad was "I'm sorry, "I am so sorry". His emotions were getting the best of him, and I could feel his pain and sorrow through the phone.

Things were a blur for those first few days. The number of people who started showing up at our house was amazing. Apparently, some of our friends went around the neighborhood telling our neighbors what had happened. They came out in full force full of hugs, food, and drink. I am not sure why people thought they needed to bring something when they came to the house, but most of them did.

Within thirty minutes after hearing of the accident, Char received a phone call from the American Red Cross. Both Mom and Jenelle had signed up to be organ donors. Apparently, the Red Cross needed lots of medical information as soon as possible to be able to retrieve the organs from their bodies that would help others. So, here we were filled with emotions thinking about Jenelle and Amy while the Red Cross was preparing to cut them open to retrieve parts of their bodies to help others. Talk about additional stress!

I was glad that they called Char, not me. I probably would have hung up on them. Char took the time, approximately thirty minutes, to answer their questions. I am glad that she did. It continues to be important to us to know that Jenelle, Amy, and Mom continue to live in this world through the body of other human beings. It comforts us to know that parts of them are still alive and helping others to live. Thank you, American Red Cross, for making this happen.

About two hours after we learned of their death, we still hadn't seen our son, Matt. He was supposed to be at football practice, but for some reason he had skipped it that day. We sent friends out to look for him, but they couldn't find him. This was just another thing for us to worry about. Finally, we saw Matt riding his bicycle home around 7:30 p.m. How do you tell a 16-year-old boy that his two sisters and his Grandma died earlier in the day? There is no good way to share this information, so Char and I simply gave him a big hug and told him the news.

As we go through this book, you will learn that **everybody grieves differently**. Matt really did not react at all to the news. He did not cry, he did not scream and shout, he just became quiet. To this day, Matt says that nothing bad that happens surprises him. His emotions always stay even. Is this a good thing or a bad thing? I'm not sure. It is just his way of handling grief. So, shortly after the accident, we had three people in the same family all reacting in totally different ways. Matt showed minimal emotions, Char didn't believe the girls were dead, and I cried like a baby. Yes, everybody **does grieve differently**.

How do you make decisions after hearing news like this? Whom do you call? What do you say? You have heard the saying "A mile a minute". When a person hears overwhelming news like the death of a friend or family member, a better term should be "A million miles a minute". That is how fast their brain is moving. So many questions, so many decisions to make. This is where a good friend should step up to say, "I know there are a lot of things to do, but we can do them together. I am with you, and we will get through this together". Fortunately, we had some great friends that really stepped up to help.

Our good friends were Brian and Mary Jo. They realized that we were confused and agitated. What next? What do we do now? I felt like I was falling into a large hole—with no bottom in sight. The next several hours were a complete nightmare for all of us. We decided to go to Gibson City to be with Dad and the rest of the family. Fortunately, Brian and Mary Jo realized that we were not physically capable of driving. These good friends offered to drive us, even though it was a seven-hour round trip. They stepped up to help us through this crisis, no questions asked.

Along the way to Gibson City, I had to make one of the toughest calls of my life to Jenelle's boyfriend, David. How do you explain to a nineteen-year-old boy that the love of his young life died in a car accident a few hours ago? How would this loss affect him? How would it affect the hundreds of friends that Mom, Jenelle, and Amy had? Death affects so many more people than the immediate family.

I hesitantly dialed the phone to call her boyfriend. I was surprised and greatly appreciated the fact that David's Dad answered the phone. I was glad a family member was able to explain this nightmare to his son. We were fortunate that David and his family had a strong faith. They immediately felt our pain and offered condolences. You just never know how somebody, especially a teenager, will react to this type of news. I imagine that his family was there consoling him just like our family was consoling us.

The importance of family and friends understanding grief while compassionately helping those who are grieving is extremely helpful. Please remember, if you do not know what to say, then don't say anything. A simple hug and saying that you are praying for and/or thinking of the person is more important. **HUGS HELP.**

When we arrived in Gibson City, most of my immediate family was already there. I come from a large family that includes two brothers, two sisters, and eighteen grandkids. Twenty-eight crying and confused family members met at Dad's small house to share our pain and try to figure out what was happening. As a group, we were completely lost and did not know what to do or say. After the hugs were completed, things got very quiet.

Char chose to try to sleep. I needed to take a walk. It was 2:00 in the morning and I was out walking around Gibson City. I remember yelling, cussing, throwing things, and non-stop crying. Fortunately, my brothers, Gary, and Scott, followed me from a distance. I did not know what they thought I would do, but thankfully, they chose to stay way behind me and leave me alone.

The next day, we all drove to the crash site. Our best friends Dave and Patti picked us up early in the morning. It is hard to describe our thoughts and feelings as we stopped at the exact spot where our daughters and Mom died less than a day before. I remember us all trying to imagine what had happened and what we could have done to prevent it. By the time we arrived, somebody had already created three wooden crosses and hung them on a telephone pole to honor mom and the girls. It was a very thoughtful gesture.

A stranger added three crosses and some flowers at the accident site.

We scoured the area and found some pieces of the wrecked car as well as some personal belongings of the girls. At the crash site we found Mom's glasses, Amy's color crayons and several of the items that Grandma Jean had just purchased for the girls. We brought these items home and hung on to them for several years. At this time, we were all just thinking this was a terrible accident and did not realize what had happened. We later learned that this was much more than an accident—PURE STUPIDITY—is what cost the lives of Jenelle, Amy, and Mom.

Warning signs or Gifts from God?

Do people have premonitions about death before they die?

Amy was nine and yet she wanted us to lay by her every night at bedtime. In fact, many times she would lay on us and just listen to our heartbeat. She did not like to be alone. One time Char and Amy flew to Florida for a vacation and the rest of us drove there. Amy asked Char what would happen if the plane crashed? Char calmly said, "Then we will go to heaven together". That was enough reassurance for Amy to be happy.

A few days before Amy died, she drew a "silly picture" for her friend. It showed a country road, a big sign that said STOP and three zigzags in the sky that said DEATH. Wow. Our neighbor showed us the drawing a few weeks after the girls had died. There was no doubt in our minds that Amy knew she was going to die.

This is Amy at age 9, right after her 3rd grade graduation.

When Jenelle was in high school, she wrote notes to herself. One was a list of things she wanted to do before she reached 21. For instance, "Have a steady boyfriend by age 21". Jenelle then folded the paper up small and wrote on the outside "Do not open unless I die". Maybe this was just a teenager wanting privacy. Char thinks Jenelle had a premonition.

In April 2003, Char started getting a strong feeling that one of our daughters was going to die. She would ask God, "Which daughter do you need"? She felt both girls were good Christians and were "ready". Char had this same feeling more than once before their deaths. Was this a premonition or a sign from God?

Another good friend of ours dreamed her husband had died. She woke up, went downstairs, and was thrilled to find him sitting in the kitchen eating ice cream. He died a few months later after being murdered a co-worker.

It is possible we receive messages or warning signs. We just need to take our dreams and premonitions to heart.

The news of an accident and of any death affects people in many ways. Below are a couple of stories family members shared with me.

Char's thoughts on what happened on July 22, 2003

The day we learned that Jean, Jenelle, and Amy had died messed up my mind. My first thought was the coroner was lying. He had the wrong family. Maybe Jean had died, but she would not allow harm to come to Jenelle and Amy. Her job, after ours, was to protect her grandchildren. I DID NOT BELIEVE THEY WERE DEAD!

The coroner asked Randy to call someone. Randy called his dad and talked. Then he called our good friends Brian and Mary Jo Reed. They immediately came over.

Randy started crying upon hearing the news from the coroner. I did not shed a single tear. I was in deep shock. Randy asked me to call my mom and dad. I refused. If I called them, then my daughters' deaths would be real. Jean would really have died. Jenelle and Amy would be DEAD; the "no coming back ever dead." This was not possible. Randy and I had done everything right. We were cautious parents. We attended church every Sunday and loved God with our whole hearts.

When our friends arrived, they were crying. Mary Jo looked scared when she saw me because she thought I had died in the accident instead of Randy's mom. I just said, "It was Randy's mom". We hugged and sat on the sofa. Randy and Brian went into another room. I immediately told Mary Jo that I thought suicide was an option for me. She begged me to let her know before taking such an action. I did agree to call her if I continued to feel suicidal. That was the end of that conversation. Just knowing that someone cared enough about me put an end to any more thoughts of suicide. I knew that suicide destroys families and that ending my life really was not the answer to my problems. Mary Jo also came over daily after that to check on us.

Since that day, a high school classmate of mine lost her only son to a freak accident. When we met in person with other friends, we both said the thought of killing ourselves crossed our mind. Fortunately, the feeling does not last.

People who lose loved ones want the pain to go away. The thought of suicide does cross people's mind. This is something family members and friends need to be aware of and watch out for in friends who have suddenly lost children, spouses or other loved ones.

I called co-workers of mine who were also great friends. Jayne and Barb came over as fast as possible. They hugged me and asked if I had told our neighbors. I had not, so they set about the task of telling our neighbors.

Randy said if I did not call my parents, he would. Therefore, I reluctantly called my dad and mom. Because it was a Tuesday evening, mom was at a church meeting. Therefore, dad answered, and I said hi and that I had bad news. I said Jenelle, Amy and Jean had died in a car accident. I still did not really believe what I had said. I then called my brother Jim and told him the news. He, in turn, called my other family members. My family is not very emotional. I am sure dad, Jim and others were all in shock and all my dad could say was "That is just terrible".

My mother did not take the news well and an EMT had to be called to monitor her health while she tried to absorb the loss of two grandchildren.

Our son, Matt, was seventeen and remembers the following about that day.

"I was at the mall when Brian Reed found me and told me to head home immediately. I had no idea what was going on and I found my dad sitting on the front porch when I arrived at the house. He gave me a big hug and told me what had happened to my sisters and grandma. I could not believe it was true and really did not know how to feel or react. I remember Mary Jo and the coroner taking me downstairs and telling me exactly what happened. I remember him describing Jenelle and Amy as "squished beyond recognition". I remember meeting with the cousins at Grandpa's home later that evening. One of my cousins asked me if I would be getting "Jenelle's and Amy's money". It was obvious that he did not understand what was happening.

Matt recalls that it took one week or longer for him to realize that both of his sisters were dead. He was so used to seeing Amy around the house. Not seeing her daily, made him finally realize that he would never see her again. He immediately started worrying about Char and me. We were not eating. He worried about our health. He worried about money and thought that we might lose our house. Matt admits that he tries not to think about the girls and prefers to concentrate on positive versus negative thoughts.

Below is a note from my sister Jill Reid, about how she learned of our family's tragedy.

"Memories of that day seep into my thoughts frequently; memories that seem as fresh as the day of the accident. I remember the day very well. At least what I was doing right before I got 'the call' and the several hours after.

It was a beautiful, sunny, warm July day. My three youngest kids were at bible school and my eleven-year-old was home, playing video games in the basement. I had been outside painting the swing set that my dad had made for all five of us kids one Christmas. I needed a break and went inside; I sat down at my desk in the office. A few minutes later, the phone rang. I answered with my usual "Hello, Reid's". A female voice on the other end of the line said that she was calling from the McClain County Sheriff's Office and that she was calling to tell me that there had been an accident. I remember picking up a pen and writing down "Mom, Amy, and Jenelle" as she was telling me about the accident – I guess I was expecting to write down what hospital they had gone to or what sort of injuries they had. The words that came next altered my life forever; "I'm so sorry. They were all killed in the accident." I remember saying, "What? What did you say?" She repeated the news. Since there was nothing else to write down, I remember dropping my pen.

A sort of panic set in after that – a weird sort of panic. I started picking up items in my already clean house. I called a friend to ask her to pick up my child that was home – I was not ready to tell him yet. I remember that phone call too. My friend was out but her husband answered the phone. I said, "There has been a tragedy in my family. Please come and pick up Nate." He responded, "I'll be right there", no further questions asked. I yelled down the stairs, "Nate, Kevin wants you to come over and play. His dad is picking you up. Please wait for them in the driveway."

I continued to roam through the house aimlessly. My chest hurt – I took two chewable aspirin. I debated whom to call but I did not want to say the words aloud. It was as though saying it would make it real. I was in disbelief. How could this happen? This was not happening! It must be a mistake. Life will never be the same.

My husband was on a work trip out of state; I finally called him and told him the unimaginable. He choked up and said he would get the next flight out and be home as soon as he could. He called his mom and stepdad and they headed to my house. I called my neighbor and a good friend. They called a couple of people, including the pastor of my church. Soon, I had a house full of people. People who did not know quite what to say or do, but who knew the value of their presence. Someone brought the kids home from Bible School and my oldest home from his friend's house. They did not know why there were so many people at the house, and they were extremely concerned. I was afraid they would think something happened to their dad, so I decided I needed to tell them. I took them down into the finished basement to give us all a little privacy. Then I told them; "Grandma, Amy and Jenelle were killed in a car accident. A truck driver was not paying attention and blew through a stop sign hitting their car." Each of them responded differently. The two youngest, who were only six years old, both cried and clung to me. The second oldest, who was very close to Grandma Jean and only four days apart in age from Amy, curled up in a ball on the floor and sobbed. The oldest looked sad but went over and started playing a video game; he did not say anything right away. We were all heartbroken.

A bit later, I was sitting upstairs with the company that had gathered when my six-year-old daughter Megan came over to me and said, "Mommy, I need to tell you something." She then leaned over and whispered in my ear, "I see Grandma and Amy and Jenelle – they are standing over there" and she pointed to an area behind me, near the window. Then she said, "Now they are over there," pointing to another area, before going back to what she had been doing. I looked. I looked again. In addition, at that moment I felt a little bit of comfort; my mom and my two beautiful nieces were gone **but not GONE**.

I remember someone trying to explain Megan's 'vision' to me, saying that she said that because she 'missed them'. However, she had just heard about their deaths. At age six, she really did not even have a good grasp on the permanency of death. Once we had gathered at my dad's house, I told my family what Megan said, and what she saw. Many stated it gave them some comfort.

Awaiting three funerals was surreal. Many friends and relatives stopped by my dad's house, where our family had gathered first, awaiting my mom's funeral. There were many tears. In addition, there was laughter. We laughed at pictures and the memories they evoked. Then we cried, knowing we would never be able to create any newer memories with them. The children in the house understood there was great sadness but were still children who needed to run and play and giggle. People dropped off enough food to feed an army; I guess some considered our large family an army of sorts and that we needed food. I'm not sure we ever actually sat the kids down to feed them the days we were at my dad's – I think they grazed on the foods that were brought over, knowing not to complain but to make do. After all, what child would not take the opportunity to have cookies for breakfast?

A carload of us drove to the accident site, about 20 minutes from my dad's house. We wanted, maybe needed, to see where it happened. To see where our loved ones took their last breaths. Someone had put three crosses at the accident site. We later learned that the man who was the first to come upon the scene of the accident, who had stopped to help, but soon realized there was nothing he could do, added these beautiful crosses. His thoughtfulness was touching. I remember looking around the accident site for a cross necklace that my mom always wore. It had the teeth marks of my oldest child, who had left this permanent reminder of himself when he was a baby, sitting on his grandma's lap. At that moment I was frantic to find this necklace; I wanted it around my own neck, a reminder of my mom and my children's grandmother. We decided that the grandchildren should attend their grandmother's wake briefly; a good friend of the family offered to take all 14 of them to their house afterward. My kids excitedly told me what fun they had with their cousins at this friend's house; they ate pizza and had candy! Small pleasures in the context of great grief...

There was a huge line of people at my mom's wake. I remember thinking how much that would have pleased her! The stories those in line told us supported what we already knew about our mom; she was a happy, vibrant, selfless, always smiling woman. Friends shared touching stories and crazy antics; we cried, and we laughed. We craved for more stories about the mom we loved and would miss the rest of our lives.

Mom's funeral was beautiful. I know it seems odd to describe a funeral as beautiful, but that is what it was. Filled with gorgeous flowers, words of hope, stories of the amazing life she lived, and music sung by Jake's Boys, a group of men who had come together when my mom determinedly sought each of them out a few years earlier when she put together a local production of Joseph and the Amazing Technicolor Dreamcoat. She would have been so pleased that they came together to sing at her funeral.

I do not remember going to the cemetery after the funeral. I only remember the beautiful flowers; reading the cards from those who sent them; and trying to decide what to do with so many flowers! One funeral down, two more to go. Unfathomable but true. I have fewer memories of the next few days; I do not know if it is because my overloaded mind and heart were so full of grief, or if my mind was simply protecting me from the horrors of seeing two young girls laid to rest. Whichever it is, I wish I remembered more; more than just seeing the girls in their caskets; my grief-stricken brother, sister-in-law and nephew standing beside them. I can still picture Amy in her casket, more so than my mom or Jenelle. It still haunts me.

The days that followed the deaths and funerals of my mom and two nieces are not as clear either. I remember seeing plants, flowers, and cards with meaningful written words arriving at my house. I remember friends bringing over food. Moreover, I remember doing things like putting the cleaning solution in the fridge and the milk in the cabinet. My mind was mush. Thoughts were unclear. Tears were frequent. Life seemed to be moving in a constant state of blur.

Day by day, month-by-month, year by year…. Time passed. Tears became less frequent but have never completely ceased. I became able to speak of the accident and the loss of my mom and nieces without breaking down; something that took years to happen. I do believe that, although our family survived this tragedy, we have never been the same. Mom was the clear matriarch of our family. She planned the events. She led the fun. She was our common link. The bond that kept our family glued tightly together. Jenelle and Amy were high spirited, fun, smiling girls who loved life. The three who loved life the most were taken from us, leaving us to our own devices to navigate this tricky world. No fun 'cousin time' anymore with Jenelle and Amy. No advice from my mom on how to handle the rough spots of childrearing and marriage. One man's careless moments on the road cost us a lifetime without mom, Jenelle, and Amy.

My older brother, Gary, shared the following about how he learned about the accident.

"The four of us had just finished supper. We had recently disconnected the old answering machine and were in the habit of ignoring the landline wall phone. This time I picked up the phone after a few rings. The caller identified herself as the McLean County Coroner. She quickly identified herself, said she had bad news and reported the crash that killed

Mom, Jenelle, and Amy. I remember repeating the words: "Oh, my" many times. I composed myself and asked my wife to join me in another room. As I shared the words 'were killed', she melted into a crying hysteria. After some semblance of recovery, we gathered our children, ages 18 and 10 on a couch and shared the news. Again, upon the words "were killed" my wife and daughter broke into hysterical tears. The 10-year old's reaction was one of confusion.

How do you pack for three sudden funerals? How do you console a sibling who has just lost two young daughters? Whom do you call first? How do you stop crying? The evening and following days are still mostly a blur. As we stumbled through that evening trying to think through the trauma, notifications, and traveling for three funerals over the next many days, there was no semblance of any order to the process. We just reacted. To this day, I can remember only a few of the conversations and phone calls that took place at our house.

Randy did call and all I just kept crying and kept repeating: "your girls, your girls".

I asked one of my nieces what she remembered most about the funerals. Her story goes as follows:

There was a bench of sorts in a room just to the left of Grandma's casket. I could still see the line of people from where I sat on this bench. Then, my cousins—mostly girl cousins—were coming through the line behind me. One by one, they sat on the bench with me, or on top of me. It was both a very sad moment as well as a beautiful one. I held this image in my head as one of both hope and love and peace because I know that it made Grandma Jean smile.

Our good friends, Brian and Mary Jo were with us that day and shared the following thoughts:

On a regular Tuesday afternoon while I was working on a scrapbook project, my husband, Brian received a call from Randy down the road. The call was short, and when he hung up, Brian exclaimed urgently that he was going to Randy's because "something was wrong with him!" What? What do you mean? I asked. I said, "I'm coming too!" We immediately dashed out the door and drove the couple of blocks through the neighborhood to Randy and Char's house. Thereupon, we were met by a man walking toward us as we were exiting our car; it turns out it was the local coroner whom we recognized. He informed us of what situation we were walking into. Nothing could prepare us for presenting ourselves as "first responders" to friends who require support in this unthinkable tragedy. For a moment, I was confused on who had passed away as the coroner spoke simultaneously while we approached the front door of their house. I heard him say the girls had passed and their mother too, who would be my dear friend, Char! Then as the door opened and we grabbed hugs of desperation with Randy, Char appeared from behind the door, and I shrieked in relief! The relief was short-lived, replaced with the ugly truth that Jenelle, Amy, and Randy's mom, Jean, all died in an automobile accident.

Who prepares for a moment like this? I dare say, not I! At the raw beginning, I am not sure there are any correct words. Only hugs, tears, shock, disbelief and more of the same. They needed someone to sweep up the glass when Char shakily dropped a water glass while dealing with the shock. By later in the evening, we began to think about what is practical, and that we needed to get Randy, Char, and Matt to Gibson City where Randy's father lived, and his family was going to be meeting. Randy was not in any shape to make the 3 ½ hour drive. We arranged for overnight care for our sons, then thirteen and ten years old, with my sister, and met the Stockers for piling into our van. It was perhaps around 10 pm now, so it would be a dark, miserable drive in every aspect of the word. No manner of preparation could help us help them. We felt at a loss, but in the troubled silence, we hoped our presence was somehow a smidgen of relief. Char had to relieve her aching gut of the stomach contents stirred by shock and disbelief – that happened halfway through our drive. I remember thinking that physical pain that the girls and Jean might have experienced would bother Randy and Char, so I attempted my first words of comfort and told them in my experience being in a car accident in college, that despite my bruises, I had experienced no pain.

As stupid as it sounds, I wanted to find something positive. However, reality truly had us at a loss –we just hugged and cried more when we dropped Char and Randy off at his dad's house about 1:30 in the morning. We then headed to a friend of their family's house for part of a night's sleep.

We went home to Quincy the next day, our kids and jobs calling and in the knowledge that Char, Randy, and Matt were where they needed to be with all their siblings and family surrounding them.

I cannot remember how the days went by after the funerals. I hope we were helpful as friends/neighbors. Time is necessary for grief. We checked on our neighbors frequently. We were not strangers to losing a daughter. Ours was under very different circumstances. Our first child, baby Allison, never left the hospital after a 3- hour life. We had been aware of the diaphragmatic hernia since around 5 month's gestation. Much of our grief took place while our baby grew in utero, as we knew she had very little chance of survival. We knew the pain of giving a child back to Jesus, but not of loving them in our own home, making memories, and watching them grow.

Therefore, while it felt hard and nearly impossible to find comforting words for the Stockers, we connected through sharing our personal loss. We knew each "first" after the girls and "mom" died would be the hardest.

It had to have been through one of our many conversations that Christmas came up. Char and Randy shared that they felt incapable of sitting in their normal front pew at St. Peter's Catholic Church, fearing the memories of past Christmases with the family intact. All the regular holiday traditions the Stocker family had formed as Quincy residents were too painful to reenact. Thus, we began attending Christmas Eve mass at Blessed Sacrament parish instead of attending St. Peter's. Randy, Char, and Matt began coming to our house for soup and dessert before services each year. This new tradition of having the Stocker family lasted for many years after; having the Stocker family with us on Christmas Eve, and with the addition of Melissa once she was adopted into their family. Char and Randy made the personal decision to have us attend Christmas mass at our own parish the following years, but I know that was quite a feat in the first years.

One time that I offered to bring lunch and join Char at their business, I made a mistake and bought Arby's sandwiches. I learned after the fact this was Jenelle's favorite fast food. Char had avoided the pain of revisiting Arby's unbeknownst to me. I felt horrible about the sad mood I triggered, but I knew Char would not "unfriend" me; rather she was grateful for lunch with a friend.

We were able to share with Char and Randy over the next years how proud we were of them for all the positive steps they were taking in their grief. I know that they grieve to this day, but the process of healing was a frequent topic of conversation amongst Brian and myself with Randy and Char. It was a reality that they lived with, and there was no "sweeping it under the rug." After losing our baby, my therapy consisted mainly of making a thick and detailed scrapbook of "everything Allison". It was the only part of her that we had left with us, and once completed I often gave my scrapbook a hug with my otherwise empty arms. With our good friends, their situation consisted of much more. We helped make decisions about years of photographs, memories, and personally owned or created items by the girls. My heart ached for them.

When they began to speak about the possibility of adopting another child, we encouraged Char and Randy! They had been the loving, doting mom, and dad, routinely in the backyard playing with their kids, all the games that kids love to play. So much laughter had taken place in the Stocker home. Nothing changed the fact that these parents had "too much love" and needed to offer it to some abundantly blessed little one! After our loss, God blessed Brian and me with two energetic and healthy birthed sons. We thought of this as nothing other than a godsend that they were ready to consider adoption and have a new sister for Matt. Eventually, Melissa and Matt became the focus of those doting parents, never forgetting Jenelle, Amy, and Grandma Jean who would have loved seeing the family regroup and live a grateful life.

It is impossible to put into words the lengthy process of moving forward. To this day, we thank God for giving Char and Randy the grace to do just so. We wanted the best for our friends, but we were unable to help them go around, under, or over their grief; because we knew they had to go THROUGH it. We hope we helped a little. We did not really know how to make it easier for them. We just tried to listen and find something positive to offer even if it was only our shoulder when they cried. We have come full circle with our joy for the Stocker family to live and love after brutal circumstances. Randy and Char have exemplified that when life "breaks you", it is not over. We know they have experienced some new beginnings and some joyful purposes because they allowed God to transform them and to find their new life worth living.

Section 1

What is grief?

Hugs Help Cure Tears

To be able to help someone who is grieving, you need to have a good understanding of what grief is and how grief can and will affect somebody. Below are two quotes about grief.

Grieving is as natural as
Crying when you are hurt,
Sleeping when you are tired,
Eating when you are hungry
Or sneezing when your nose itches.

A cut finger
Is numb before it bleeds
It bleeds before it hurts
It hurts before it begins to heal,
It forms a scab and itches until
Finally, the scab is gone and
A small scar is left where
There was once a wound.
Grief is the deepest wound
You have ever had.

I found both sayings in the Grief and Bereavement Ministry pamphlet created by the Office for Family and Youth Ministry in Springfield, IL. The first saying tries to simplify grief, even though it is not a simple emotion. The second poem does a good job of explaining how grief can start as a minor emotion and then continue to grow into the biggest pain a person has ever suffered.

Chapter 1

Grief – Key Words to Know

What exactly is grief? There are several definitions including:

- Grief is the intense spiritual and emotional suffering that people go through when faced with a loss or the possibility of a loss.
- Grief is an internal reaction in the form of thoughts and emotions.
- Grief just happens and is nearly impossible to control.
- Grief is an active word, which describes the many symptoms such as feelings, beliefs, and thoughts as we remember and reflect on our loss.
- Grief is both an unconscious and conscious response by our body, mind, and soul.

CS Lewis had a quote about grief being a natural and human reaction to death. He also talked about the pain we now suffer from is caused by a previous happiness that we experienced. Grievers are reacting now from the happiness and joy they experienced with their loved ones in the past. They are thinking about the many good times they have already gone through and are frustrated and grieving because they realize they will not be able to experience those same feelings again in the future.

There are numerous types or models of grief. Some of them include:

- **Anticipatory grief** is the process where a person plans to grieve in advance of a death. This occurs more when the person is sick, and a probable death is imminent.

Because we suffered from the sudden death of our daughters, we did not struggle with this type of grief. Because of this, we are much more nervous about something bad happening again to our family or us. Once you have lost, especially with a sudden loss, you cannot help but expect it to happen again.

- **Complicated grief** is like being in an ongoing, heightened state of mourning that keeps you from healing. Some of the symptoms of complicated grief that were most hurtful to us included:
  – Our intense sorrow
  – Our intense pain and suffering over their loss
  – Our total lack of focus on little else but their death.
  – Our lack of meaning or purpose in life.
  – Our bitterness about our loss and anger towards others that were enjoying their lives, despite our loss.
  – Our withdrawal or failure to participate in activities or events that we always enjoyed attending.

Jenelle was nineteen and Amy was only nine when they died. We had some amazing and memorable experiences with them during their short lifetimes. We never wanted nor expected the fun times to ever end with our daughters. After their death, we started thinking about all the future events that we would be missing. Some of the key events we knew would now never happen that hurt the most were:

- Not being able to attend graduations. We saw Jenelle's High school graduation and Amy's third grade event. Those were the last two we would ever see for them. I remember when I attended my niece Kristen's college graduation in May 2008. Although I was so proud of Kristen for what she had accomplished, I cried through the ceremony just thinking that I should be attending my own daughter's college graduation as well. It was an event and a joy that I will never be able to experience.
- Not being able to walk my daughters down the aisle. Jenelle had a boyfriend—a great person named David. Maybe they would have gotten married. We will never know. I remember attending

my best friend's daughter's wedding in 2010. All I could think about is the fact that I was never going to walk Jenelle or Amy down the aisle. That is what a father is supposed to do. I remember practicing walking her down the aisle, just as something fun that a father and daughter could do. We would sing the wedding song together and then hug at the end of the aisle. It was so much fun thinking about the bright future that both Jenelle and Amy had.

- Not being able to have grandkids—who knows if either Jenelle or Amy would have had children—we would like to think they would have. Their death has most likely prevented several other children from being born into this world. We were so fortunate that our son Matt and his girlfriend Sierra gave us twin grandsons in 2020. My parents had eighteen grandchildren. Char and I were hoping for at least five. With the loss of Jenelle and Amy, the pressure is on Matt and Melissa. It is amazing that the pure stupidity of one person can cause the loss of a bright future for so many.

When we grieve, it is not because love has been lost. We will always have love in our hearts for those who have died. We grieve because the person we love has been taken from our life. We will miss their hugs, we will miss their friendship, and we will miss their conversations. Not only do we miss what we had, we miss what we will now never have. Our future memories and plans have been shattered and destroyed.

I wished that it had been me who was killed in that accident instead of Jenelle and Amy. I was 45 years old and had a good life. These two were so young. Why didn't I die instead of them?

Losing a loved one is one of the most distressing and painful experiences that people face. Some people go through a period of pain and sorrow, and then accept the loss and move on. Others, like us, did not see our grief or pain decrease for a long period. Instead, we would wake up each day realizing that our daughters were dead, and that this new day would be just like the previous day—filled with pain and sadness. We were not sure for a long time whether we would even survive our loss, much less recover from it. We went to grief counselors and learned some things about how to control our grief.

Some of the key points learned included:

- Learning to accept the reality of our loss.
- Taking the time needed to express our unbearable grief and pain by letting our emotions out.
- Realizing what Mom, Jenelle, and Amy would have wanted us to do with our lives. They would want us to find a way to be happy without them in our lives.

It probably took us an entire year to fully understand and live with our grief. When we took our extended family on a vacation to Disney World on the anniversary of the accident, we decided at that time that we could have fun and enjoy life to a small extent without the girls. Was it hard? Absolutely. Was it beneficial? Yes, it was.

From what I have read, it is extremely hard to prevent complicated grief. We recommend the following actions to help:

1. **Talk about your grief.** Talking about your grief and allowing yourself to cry also can help prevent you from being stuck in your sadness. As painful as it is, trust that in most cases, your pain will start to lift if you allow yourself to feel it.
2. **Ask for Support.** Family members, friends, social support groups and your faith community are all good options to help you work through your grief. You may be able to find a support group focused on a particular type of loss, such as the death of a spouse or a child. Ask your doctor to recommend local resources.
3. **Attend bereavement counseling.** Through early counseling after a loss, you can explore emotions surrounding your loss and learn healthy coping skills. This may help prevent negative thoughts and beliefs from gaining such a strong hold that they are difficult to overcome.

Disenfranchised grief happens when a loss is not or cannot be openly acknowledged, publicly mourned, or socially supported. An example is a doctor who cannot openly grieve for the loss of his or her patients.

A good friend of mine is a medical professional and has struggled with her grief for years. She described her grief below:

"The most helpful thing I ever learned about grieving was that grief is like a ball in a box. Inside the box, there is a pain button. Initially, the ball is as big as the entire box so that the pain button is constantly pressed. Over time, the ball gets smaller. It starts bouncing around in the box. Sometimes this pain button is not being pressed. But then, with no warning, the ball may bounce and hit the pain button. Sometimes the ball gets bigger again; sometimes the ball goes days without hitting the pain button. However, the pain button never truly goes away.

As a medical professional, she shares her perspective of both being a healthcare provider, and from what she has witnessed in grieving families.

Healthcare professionals also all grieve differently. What has worked for me is to bury it deep/build a wall approach. I have had to sit with a mother as she cradles her dying child in her arms...and in the next half hour, I had to joke around with a teenager and his family as he recovered from surgery. I have been in the room when kids have died. The howling, keening noise their parents make never truly leaves you. For me, to survive this emotional rollercoaster, remain professional, and still help others requires that I bury my own emotions and grief as deep as I possibly can.

According to her, the healthcare professional:

1. Everyone grieves differently. If you are the person trying to help, ask before giving a hug.
2. Do not ask what you can do to help. Brains do not function well under acute grief, so asking hurts more than it helps.
3. Provide concrete assistance. Bring them food. A change of clothes. House sit. Pick up the other kids from school. Get the chaplain to sit with them. Stock their fridge. Walk the dog.

4. Do not push your own grief onto those experiencing the loss most acutely.
5. Therapy is necessary.
6. Siblings grieve too. Utilize child life, chaplains, therapy dogs, and sibling support groups whenever able.
7. Sometimes a fast death is the less painful one over time.
8. A good death can be a beautiful thing.

Never being a medical professional, I truly appreciate the thoughts about grieving from my friend. Her mention about a fast death for Mom and the girls was hard to read, but fully understandable. She stated that she was glad they died that day only because traumatic brain injuries make horrible, drawn-out deaths for families, where unimaginable decisions have to be made, choices that would hurt as much as or more than the grief itself. She has seen instances of TBI (Traumatic brain injuries) that have been like a living death for otherwise vibrant and creative people.

As the father of Jenelle and Amy, and the son of Jean, I have often thought about what our lives would be like if they had not all died on that terrible July day. This is something to consider when you are discussing loss with your friends. Maybe it is true that sometimes a good death can be a beautiful thing.

- **Dysfunctional grief** happens when we do not follow the five typical steps of grieving (denial, anger, bargaining, depression, and acceptance) in order.
  I have mentioned before that nobody grieves in the same manner or pattern. In my opinion, all grieving is dysfunctional grieving. It would be excessively easy if we all grieved in the same manner for the exact same amount of time. This just does not make any sense.
- **Masked grief** occurs when the person experiencing the grief claims that they are not grieving. Instead, they mask their feelings, hiding their grief from others. Our culture sometimes dictates or mandates how we must act or what we must do when grieving. The peer pressure to "quit crying or get on with your life" sometimes causes us to "mask or hide our grief".

In our case, there was pressure to hide our grief and get back to work. Char did a much better job of hiding her grief than I did. We both felt more comfortable crying in a private setting than in a public one.

- **Prolonged Grief** has several risk factors and causes. These risks tie into the health and well-being of the survivor prior to the loss, the relationship, and to the nature of the death. Individuals who have experienced an unexpected or violent death of a loved one may be at greater risk of suffering prolonged grief and are more likely to have mental issues like depression.
- **Shadow Grief** is a "dull ache in the background of one's feelings that remains fairly constant or on occasion, starts to grow". Occasionally, this grief comes spewing to the top in the form of anger, violence, and rage.

Even eighteen years later, I feel that shadow grief occasionally progresses up my system until I explode. It is hard to explain, but I can feel the grief within me build up and continue to grow inside of me. This usually results in a panic attack or a terrible fit of anger and emotion. This was most obvious during the early years. I was taking some strong depression medicine. Occasionally, I decided that I was strong enough to survive without medication. I was wrong. I would not say that I became suicidal, but I sure was not much fun.

Other key terms associated with death and grieving include:

- **Bereavement** refers to suffering from the loss of someone we love—because they died. It is a time of being "deprived" of that which we have valued.
- **Depression** is a feeling or condition marked by hopelessness and self-doubt. It affects how one thinks, feels, and reacts to daily life. I look at depression as the next step after grieving. The unyielding loss of hope caused by sudden death led us directly into depression. Nothing was going right. It was a real struggle to make any decision. We had such an amazing future planned with Jenelle and Amy that disappeared in the blink of an eye.

Persistent negative thoughts and feelings are common for people with depression. Some of the many symptoms that we experienced include:

- Feelings of hopelessness, helplessness, or pessimism
- Feelings of worthlessness, guilt
- Feeling tired, run-down, having low energy
- Loss of interest or pleasure in activities
- Problems concentrating, thinking clearly, or making decisions
- Changes in sleep patterns
- Appetite changes; weight gain or loss
- Thoughts or plans of death or suicide

Not everyone with depression experiences all these symptoms. Symptoms vary among individuals and according to the stage of disease.

Depression is the result of many factors including genetic, biological, psychological, and environmental conditions.

Depression is treatable. In most cases, treatment involves a combination of psychotherapy, medications, and self-care techniques. Self-care strategies include setting realistic goals, educating yourself about depression and its treatment, postponing important decisions, managing expectations for recovery, and allowing others to help you.

Children and teens experiencing depression are often sad or irritable. They may have crying spells or become withdrawn. Anxiety and school problems are common. It can be difficult to determine whether a child is depressed or going through a difficult developmental phase, and the symptoms of depression may change as the child matures and develops. If your child or teen seems depressed, I encourage you to get a professional diagnosis and set up a treatment plan.

It is sometimes difficult to determine if a child is depressed or just acting like a teenager. Our son, Matt, just went quiet after his sisters were killed. We did not know what to do or who to talk with about his silence. We thought he was doing fine because we never saw him crying or acting depressed. What we learned later was that his way of responding to this loss was to keep his pain bottled up.

Depression is different from anxiety disorders. Unfortunately, some people have symptoms of both conditions. Nervousness, problems sleeping, irritability, and difficulty concentrating can be symptoms of both conditions. Other symptoms of anxiety disorder include muscle tension, worrying, feeling "on edge," and restlessness.

Difficult situations in life can cause a person to feel sad, scared, or anxious as a normal reaction to life's stressors. Nevertheless, people with depression experience these feelings almost every day for no apparent reason, so much so that it can affect or compromise their ability to function. Depression affects the way one thinks, feels, and functions in all aspects of life.

- **Mourning**–is the outward expression of our internal grief. Many people get the terms grief and mourning mixed up. I have heard the term "mourning" described as "grief going public". It begins the process of healing. While managing and controlling grief is nearly impossible, using mourning as a response to grief can be helpful. We try to create a new relationship with our loved one by adapting to our new world. There is a saying that "sometimes mourning is where something good comes from something bad". Mourning is both a painful and a healthy process. It is hurtful because it reinforces the realities that death has occurred in your life. It is healthy because it offers many moments or aspects of healing.
- **Sudden death** occurs when a loved one dies suddenly. The griever never got the chance to say goodbye and might continually punish themselves for words or actions left either unsaid or undone. The fact that Jenelle and Amy died suddenly has haunted me for years. The day they were leaving to go to Grandpa and Grandma's house, I was on a business call and did not take the time to give them a goodbye hug. I truly wish that I had given my daughters a proper goodbye. I will regret this decision for the rest of my life.

Chapter 2

Is Grief a Sickness?
Will I ever be happy again?

Before their death, our family was a happy one. We ate together, played sports together, went to church together, sang together (not very well) and truly enjoyed spending time together as a family. We were HAPPY.

It was hard to be happy, in any manner, after Jenelle and Amy died. Prior to their death, we would break out into songs, after their death, would break out into tears. Most of the time we even felt guilty when we were trying to have fun.

I felt sick almost all the time after we lost our daughters. I later learned that the grief emotion is so strong that it makes a person feel physically ill frequently. Both Char and I were on depression medication. She had already been taking medicine before the accident. I realized that I needed some type of help and asked my doctor to prescribe medicine for me to help "control my emotions".

Since grief is the natural response to the loss of someone we love, it is wrong to treat it as a sickness or a medical disease. The loss is permanent and poignant. Unfortunately, the grief is also eternal. You cannot cure grief with an aspirin or a Tylenol tablet. The potential health consequences related to grieving are a serious concern. If diagnosed with an illness, you would seek or wish for a cure. But thinking about grief as a disease with a cure raises questions about what is normal and abnormal about the overall experience of grieving. Is grief a condition that modern psychology, with its list of symptoms and disorders and an ample medicine cabinet, should treat as if it were an illness rather than an essential part of being human? The answer is "NO".

Medications can help control depression and hopelessness while keeping your emotions in a level area. My mind and body were all over the place those first few months. I was crying one moment, angry one moment, and nearly suicidal the next. My emotions were in a state of total confusion. The depression medicine that I took was able to help me "level off" my emotions and helped me to get through each day. If I ever forgot to take my medicine, my grief just "skyrocketed" almost immediately. That is how powerful the emotion of grief can be and how important taking the right medication is.

Sometimes men think they do not need medication because they are too tough to take it. I was that man for a while. After my third attempt to get off my depression medicine failed miserably, I made the decision to keep taking it for the rest of my life. Simply quitting taking anti-depression medicine caused me to sink into emotional despair, again. It was not worth it. I decided that if I keep taking the medicine, I would always be better off.

As you go through your own grief or if you are helping others through their grief, please keep this in mind. If your friend or family member seems to be in a "deeper than normal" rut, ask them if they are still taking their medicine.

Depending on the person involved, people can recover in many different ways from loss. Some are more adaptable and resilient and are able to recover in a shorter period. Others adapt more gradually, by following a "recovery or healing" path. The intensity of those first days, weeks and months of grieving might slowly diminish. Grievers might pick up the pieces and begin putting their lives back together, mostly because society forces them to "move on".

We suffered from complicated grief and really struggled to recover. Our grief stayed at a high level of intensity for years. Complicated grief is like being in an ongoing, heightened state of mourning that keeps you from healing. Signs and symptoms of complicated grief may include intense sorrow, pain and reflection over the loss of your loved one. It tends to last longer and stays at more intense levels. People with complicated grief focus on little else but their loved one's death.

After Jenelle and Amy died, we did not know what to do, how to act in front of people, what we needed to do privately, and who could help us. I was fearful of making people more emotional and me having to comfort them. My grief negatively affected every single aspect of my life.

Complicated grief often follows a particularly difficult loss that challenges a person's emotional, physical, and social resources. It is even worse when the mourner is deeply attached to the person they are grieving. That was so true in our case. Supposedly, it affects even more people when the death of a loved one is sudden or violent and is even more common among parents who have lost a child. Medical professionals are just beginning to acknowledge how debilitating this form of grief can be.

How often my grief slowed or accelerated was not within my control. Sometimes I would buckle and wait it out. Sometimes I would push back. Somehow, I knew it was going to take as long as it took. There was nothing that I felt I could do except take one day at a time.

Remember, everybody grieves differently. There is no set time to stop grieving. Your mind and your body will tell you when and how to shift the grief on its own or when to do something to initiate that process. You will know when to separate yourselves emotionally from the person who died so that you can regain that energy and direct it elsewhere. Do not let anybody else ever tell you how to grieve or when you should be 'over your grief'.

Chapter 3

Feelings, Emotions, and Reactions of a Griever
Will I ever stop crying?

Grief causes different feelings and emotions as well as changed behaviors in the grievers. It also affects and possibly causes different thoughts and beliefs. All of these emotions can lead to different physical symptoms.

Feelings and Emotions of Grief

Feelings. We had lots of people comment on "how strong we were" or "how poised we were in our grief". Sometimes it is more comfortable for others to imagine grief as orderly and collected vs. grotesque and messy like it really is. People who have experienced loss may have a range of feelings and sometimes feel like they are going crazy. If this is you, do not sweat it. You are probably just a normal person dealing with the unsatisfactory thoughts the grief creates in you. These include anything from shock to denial to depression. A grieving person may start crying after hearing a specific song or a comment that makes them think of the person who died. Sometimes that person may not know what triggered his or her crying.

It would not take much to set me off in a sea of tears. I would see another girl that looked like Jenelle or Amy from behind. When I realized it was not them, I would break down. Watching other people have fun and do activities with their kids would send me into crying episodes. Sitting at

13

home and looking at pictures or old videos of the girls was one of the hardest things I did. Most people thought that I cried non-stop for several months. They were almost right.

Anger. Whom do I blame for my loss? In my case, I blamed God, the truck driver, the state of Illinois, and myself. I blamed Jenelle and Amy for dying. I blamed mom for not protecting them. I got angry when people asked how I was doing, and I got angry when people did not ask how I was doing. I was angry with my wife because she would not cry. Because of my anger, I wanted to find somebody at fault for something so tragic. I blamed God because he was supposed to protect my family. I blamed the truck driver because he was speeding and reading when he killed Jenelle and Amy. I blamed myself—for making Amy go with Jenelle on this trip to see Grandpa and Grandma.

Anger is a typical emotion that occurs after the sudden death of a loved one. If the State of Illinois had installed rumble strips at that intersection where my family died, their deaths might have been prevented. In the years before our loss, several other people had died at the cross-section where the accident occurred. If they had, many more people would still be alive. Another part of anger comes from the feeling of abandonment. I was not ready to lose my mother and two daughters and felt lost without them. After the accident, I did advocate for the addition of rumble strips in this area. I believe that the media pressure along with our horrific loss were factors in getting the county to add these protective measures.

I was so angry for so long. I knew that I was "blowing up" frequently and was starting to offend people with my bouts of anger. I made the decision to purchase a punching bag and installed it in my basement. Whenever I felt the anger coming, I would go downstairs and beat the shi… out of my punching bag. This inflated bag helped me to accomplish two things—first, I was able to direct my anger and frustration towards it instead of towards friends and family. Secondly, it wore me out. Just try hitting and kicking and cussing out a large yellow bag for 30-40 minutes—it will wear you out as well.

I also got very angry with others when they were having fun. My mind kept asking, "How can these people be having fun when my daughters were recently killed?" I remember some good friends that took Char and me to a comedy club a couple of months after Jenelle and Amy died. They were just trying to help us by getting our minds off the death of our daughters. I was mentally not yet ready for this type of event. Unfortunately, I think I ruined the evening for all of us. Being angry towards others who are being happy is a "dark place" that grievers do not know how to navigate. I struggled with my navigation skills as well. I felt bad for ruining the evening, but now realize it was my grief acting out.

Bottom line—it is OK to be angry when you are grieving. Consider letting your friends know in advance that you will have good days and bad days. Ask them to be more patient with you during the bad ones.

Suicidal Thoughts. I once read that nearly four percent of Americans have thoughts of suicide. In my crazed state of mind, I could not understand why anybody else but me would ever consider hurting himself or herself. Absolutely nobody else I knew had lost his or her mom and two daughters at the same time. If anybody deserved to die, it was me.

I never took it any further than this because even though we lost Jenelle and Amy, we still had our son, Matt, at home. It would have been so selfish for me to hurt myself instead of helping others to survive. My mom was one of the strongest people I ever knew. She would have "kicked my butt" for even thinking about hurting myself. She was all about helping others—and I would be too.

If you get to this point in your grief where you are thinking about hurting yourself, please reach out to a friend, a counselor, or a family member. There is help available. The National Suicide Prevention Lifeline number is 1-800-273-8255.

Char recalls the following incident: "*We went to church together shortly after the accident. Randy left the church service early and walked home. Unfortunately, he failed to tell me that he was walking home. After church, I walked home as well, leaving the car in the church parking lot. When I arrived home, I saw that the car was not there, but Randy's billfold and phone were at the house. I was worried that he had committed suicide. Instead, Randy was in the basement struggling with his terrible emotional pain. When I did not go downstairs to check on him, he got mad at me even though I did not know he was home. Poor communication between grieving people can and will lead to more anger. In this case, Randy was angry with me because I did not check on him and I was mad at him because I thought he had hurt himself ".*

Sadness. Remembering the many good times with the girls made us both happy and sad at the same time. We were happy that we were able to remember stories about our amazing daughters, yet sad because we knew there would never be any more memories created. As a father, I had always dreamed of walking Jenelle and Amy down the aisle, attending their graduation parties, and watching their children, my future grandchildren. I do not think the pain and sadness from missing these events will ever go away. The total weight of our grief caused major sadness almost all the time.

Jealousy. I was so jealous of friends and family because they had something that I did not; their children were alive. Instead of feeling happy for them, I felt jealous and resentful. My feelings did cause some resentment from others. Fortunately, they understood that it was the grief talking and not me.

Anxiety. Char and I were totally at a loss as to what to do after we learned of the accident. Shortly afterwards, we were not capable of simple things such as driving our car around town or making such normal decisions as what to do or where to go. The stress involved in making decisions about the funeral and the visitations simply added to our anxiety.

The definition of anxiety is an apprehensive uneasiness or nervousness. To this day, I still get nervous when my family takes a trip without me. I ask myself questions like "Will I ever see them again?" "What happens if they get into an accident, and I am not there to help?" Once somebody has suffered major loss, I know from experience that their anxiety stays with them forever. If it can happen once, it can happen again. My sister, Jill, shared with me that her daughter, Megan, was terrified for her anytime she went anywhere without her. Her concern was that the same thing would happen to her mom that happened to her grandmother and her cousins.

Entitled. I still feel this way today. Life owes me something because it took away something or someone that I loved. I thought for years that I should have won the lottery simply because I lost so much and felt owed something. I would have had a better chance to win if I had purchased any lottery tickets. I am still waiting for my entitlement. Unfortunately, I now know that life does not work that way.

Denial. This is the refusal to accept the facts of the loss, either consciously or unconsciously. Refusing to deal with the consequences of the death: visiting the gravesite, getting rid of personal belongings, or even filing the necessary paperwork, prolongs the denial stage.

Char went through the denial stage for almost six months after the death of Jenelle, Amy, and Mom. She kept hoping that they were on a vacation and would be home soon. She refused to cry or grieve their loss because it was easier to deny that they were dead than to accept their deaths. It was not until Thanksgiving, 2003, that she admitted that she would never see the girls again until they all met in heaven. Then the tears began to flow.

According to the Kubler/Ross study, denial is the stage that can initially help you survive the loss. You might think life makes no sense, has no meaning, and is too overwhelming. ... Instead of becoming completely overwhelmed with grief, we deny it and do not accept it

Fear. Grief replicates fear because in some ways, it becomes our reality. If we feel it and believe it, we have just created our own eventuality. It is our worst nightmare come true.

Our fear is that an accident like this could and would happen again in the future. Our son, Matt, got in a car accident the year after his sisters died. He totaled his car, but he was OK. We both suffered major anxiety and panic until we were able to see and hug our son again. Our grief caused us to over-react to his wreck, even though he told us that he was OK.

I remember one other time when our daughter, Melissa, lost control of her car in the ice and slid into an embankment. She said that she was fine, but because of my grief, I feared the worst.

Grieving people often feel that they have lost their sense of safety and control in life, and they find themselves panicking or worrying excessively about what or whom else they could lose in the future. They also may have trouble sleeping or taking care of themselves, which can put them at higher risk for anxiety.

Helplessness. The emotions of grief and loss are very similar to those of death and dying. While the dying person must let go of everything in their lives, the grieving person must let go of having the person they love, admire, and depend on. Neither the dying person nor the grieving person can control what happens.

Helplessness is a very difficult feeling. Usually, when someone dies, we ask or torture ourselves by asking what more we could have done. The "what if" thoughts can continue for quite a while. In death by accident or suicide, the helplessness can be overwhelming. I continue to ask myself these "what-if" questions years after the loss of my family.

"What if I drove the girls to see Grandpa and Grandma? Would they still be alive?

"What if I didn't make Amy go on this trip with Jenelle? Would the accident still have happened?

"What if mom had seen that truck barreling towards them? Would she have been able to avoid the wreck?

"What if the State of Illinois had installed speed bumps at that road crossing?" Would Mom, Jenelle, Amy and many more people still be alive?

Ideally, I should have proactively shared these terrible "what if" questions with family and friends. I did not. Instead, I kept them inside of me, tearing me apart. If you find yourself in this type of situation, I encourage you to talk to others about it. The questions may not change, but it is always better to share your feelings than be all alone with them.

Shame. This is usually present in both grief and when recovering from loss. At first, I struggled with comparing our loss with the loss others had experienced. How can you not compare the devastating loss of three people to the loss of one person? I was wrong.

It took me a while to learn that every loss is a terrible loss for somebody. It does not make any sense to compare apples to monkeys but my emotions sometimes took over and I became angry at others' grief, because I felt my pain had to be worse than their pain. I still struggle comparing the loss of my nine-year old vs. the loss of an eighty-year-old. However, I am better able to handle my emotions and feelings now than I was in the past.

I took the following two-step approach when dealing with guilt and shame during my grief.

First, I tried to learn more about a particular situation versus automatically assuming my grief was worse. Secondly, I became a more compassionate person and a better listener to those who were also grieving.

Loneliness. When your life revolves around a specific person or persons and they are no longer around, you must adapt to this lack of companionship.

We had gotten used to Jenelle being away at college and just having Matt and Amy at home with us. Since Matt was a high school Junior, he did not need our involvement and preferred spending time with his friends.

Amy had just graduated from third grade. She needed constant attention, transportation, and support. Between school events, dance lessons, and soccer games, she kept us busy. We loved attending her activities and events and looked forward to spending time with her daily. Our life revolved around Amy until July 22, 2003. After that date, we were totally lost. We had more time available and did not know what to do with it. Our lifestyle changed and the loneliness we suffered through was almost unimaginable.

My dad had been married to mom for 49 years when she died. She was the leader of the house, the planner, the organizer, as well as an amazing wife, mother, and grandmother. Dad was quite lost for several months. He tried to attend the couple's events that he and mom used to attend together. However, he never felt very comfortable attending them by himself. After a while, he just stayed at home and started keeping track of the number of inbound phone calls he received. He had to do something to keep busy; he just did not know what.

At one point, dad did start dating. We were excited for him and a little bit nervous as well. I received a call from him one day that shocked the heck out of me. He said, Randy, I have started dating this woman, **and she is your age.** You know how the father is always supposed to have the talk with the son. Well, I had to have the talk with my dad. Fortunately, that relationship did not work out. A couple of years later, dad met this amazing woman, Margaret. One of Mom's best friends introduced them to each other. They started dating and really enjoyed each other's company. One September day, they called all the kids, told us they were in Las Vegas, and had gotten married. **Surprise!** Margaret has been a good person to have in my dad's life. He is no longer alone, and he is happy once again. They make an amazing couple.

The Griever's Bill of Rights-by Randy Stocker

1. You have the right to experience your own unique grief. Never let anybody tell you differently.
2. You have the right to talk about your grief.
3. You have the right to feel multiple different emotions-sometimes all at once.
4. You have the right to be tolerant of your physical and emotional limits.
5. You have the right to experience "grief bursts or blow ups". These are sudden and powerful surges of grief.
6. You have the right to make use of healing rituals and ceremonies if you so choose.

7. You have the right to embrace your religion or spirituality or the right not to embrace your religion or spirituality.
8. You have the right to search for new meaning in your life.
9. You have the right to cherish and guard your memories.
10. You have the right to "Be Happy" if you want.

'Printed with permission of GriefandSympathy.com'

GRIEF EXPECTATIONS FROM OTHERS

In our grief, it can sometimes be hard to understand the expectations of others around us. We hear things like "It is time to move-on" or are encouraged to "hide" our grief from others. Most people try to give kindhearted and well-meaning advice, but unfortunately, it occasionally makes us feel worse. Be careful in what you say. Try to use positive words and feedback to help educate your family and friends who do not fully understand what you are going through.

To the griever, grief is:

- A journey that can sometimes feel pretty messy
- Wanting to still say your deceased one's name

- Understanding that waves of emotion can and will hit you all at the same time
- Needing to give yourself a break occasionally
- Seeking out or asking for support during the tough times
- Both physically and emotionally exhausting
- A personal experience (Everybody grieves differently)
- Discovering what feels right for your grief journey
- Getting out of your comfort zone to find new friends
- Totally normal
- Allowing yourself to do what is right for you
- A judgment free zone
- Understanding that it is normal to feel bad.
- Multiple emotions all tied together
- Frustration about the inability to concentrate and make good decisions

<u>Grievers should not have to:</u>

- Ignore their feelings
- Always push-through
- Grieve the same as everyone else
- Always have good days. There can be good days as well as bad days.
- Explain why they are still grieving
- Hide their grief from others
- Grieve within a period or according to the well-known steps of grieving.
- Always do everything by themselves. Ask for help!

Chapter 4

What does time have to do with Grief?

- **<u>Does time stand still?</u>** When we are grieving, our experience has a lot to do with time. Consider the following: We all have multiple sources of seeing what time it is. Most of us keep our schedules either online or on a calendar. We have clocks in every room, most of us wear watches to keep track of time, and now, our cell phones and Apple watches are with us 24-hours per day–just to keep us on time. We never want to be late for anything. Time is precious to us.

Time appears to stand still when we are grieving. Even though we are suffering from our loss, the rest of the world keeps going, while our life has come to a screeching halt.

This feeling about the rest of the world not stopping after our loss simply drove me crazy. How can others go out to dinner and have fun? When we went, everybody we saw reminded us of our loss. How can your children still play a soccer game when my daughter is dead? How can you even consider laughing when I am crying about my loss? It just seemed like the rest of the world was very unaffected by the death of Jenelle, Amy, and Mom. It was not fair!

It made me angry. It made me frustrated. Unfortunately, it also made me act mean to others. Sometimes I lashed out at others for living life when my life had changed so much. It just was not fair. People say that time heals all wounds. That assumes the source of the grief has an end date, which it does not.

- **Time to quit grieving.** Most uninformed people give grievers a couple of weeks to maybe a full month to stop grieving. We continuously hear that it is OK to cry openly and talk about our loss for a short time–but GET OVER IT–OR IT'S TIME TO MOVE ON, was the overwhelming sentiment after that.

Why do people think there is a period to grieve? They just do not know or understand the grieving process. They were so much more comfortable being our friends before our loss and wanted us to get back to that as soon as possible. They may be thinking more of themselves than of us and may not appreciate the time it takes for us to get back to normal, (By the way, there is never a "back to normal" after a tragic loss). Think of a "new normal" that involves changing everything you do or say because someone that was a big part of your life for so long, is now gone.

Sometimes, it appears others just got tired of us dwelling on our sorrow and pain. They determined that they had given all that they could give and just did not want to be around us any longer while we were grieving.

If this happens, you may need to redefine what "normal" is for you. Choose some new friends who are willing and able to be with you on your personal grief journey and will allow you to determine yourself when your grieving time is up.

- **Looking back on time.** We spent most of our time looking back on what we had lost on July 22, 2003, at 2:22 in the afternoon. How can you not look back? It is easier to look back in time before your life changed so dramatically than to look ahead to a bleak future. It is no fun to think about what our lives would have been like in the future. Our future without Jenelle and Amy was hard to imagine.

I spent a lot of time asking myself what I could have done differently that might have saved the lives of Jenelle and Amy. What was the last thing I said to them or did with them? Did I say anything wrong or stupid? We kept talking about the "good times" and sharing stories about the girls. Memories were all we had left. There was not a future for us that involved

Jenelle and Amy. We had to keep those memories fresh in our mind so we would never forget what we lost.

- **First time.** Those first few days and weeks were very painful. Things like going to church for the first time without our daughters; trying to celebrate Father's Day or Mother's Day without Jenelle and Amy; trying to get through those first birthdays or holidays without them. We did not know if we could survive those "firsts", but we did. We determined that they were going to be extremely hard and worried about even surviving them. The anticipation leading up to these benchmark days was as hard as the actual days. I could feel pressure growing within me. I felt like I was ready to explode.

When you are grieving, your mind is out of control. My thought process kept telling me that these special days were going to be terrible. I learned over time to ignore the build-up or pressure of the days prior to the actual event. It was simply both stressing me out as well as wearing me out. We had to learn and understand that every day can be bad when you are grieving. After a while, we realized that we would be able to survive those "firsts" –whether we wanted to or not.

Speaking of the mind, one of my brothers was involved in an active shooter scenario in recent years. He was in a building when an employee in a community center in the Midwest killed his supervisor and engaged in a firefight with a police officer. He shared the story about how his mind cannot get over the fact that he did not hear 35 of the 40 gunshots. He reported his mind was fine during the event as he prepared for a variety of escape avenues. However, after learning of all the rounds fired, the unconscious brain reflexes were most troublesome.

In this case, my brother reported that his brain had unconscious processing of the realization that he had just avoided potential sudden death.

Such a reaction is like what we experienced. Our minds were running in the background and creating reactions that consumed our ability to act and react rationally. An uncontrolled mental reaction could happen if you have experienced sudden loss.

- **Jail Time.** Sometimes grieving is like being in jail. We feel imprisoned in a small space and time and just cannot set ourselves free. We do not like who we are. We do not like that our friends do not make us feel better. We just want out of jail but do not fully understand how to get away from the grief that is keeping us locked up.

At times, it felt good to be "locked up" in my grief. I was such a mean and angry person. I did not want to be around others nor hurt those who were trying to be helpful. It took me a long time to get to the point where I did not feel "confined" to my own grief.

- **Supper Time.** We went from a family of five who thoroughly enjoyed eating together to a family of three. Those two empty chairs in our dining room reminded us daily of how much we had lost. We were not able to discuss anything but our loss and our grief. That was not fair to Matt who still had his young life to live. Food was important, but seldom enjoyed. Mealtime went from an enjoyable event that the whole family looked forward to and became something that we dreaded each day.

Before the girls died, a big part of our dinnertime was for the family to eat together and share stories about their day. We would all take turns setting the table and doing the dishes afterwards. Sometimes, Jenelle and Amy would help Char cook a feast for the family. The wonderful life and times we celebrated around the table were gone for good. It was a very big adjustment. Matt started college two years later and life changed once again.

- **Time heals**. This is my last section about grieving and time. You have heard the saying about "time heals all wounds". BUNK! Time will change things, yes. The overall intensity of the grief will slowly diminish, certainly. In the years following a loss, life will slowly return. However, the saying "time heals all wounds" is just a saying. After losing three people that I loved with all my heart, I do not think that I will ever heal.

We struggled to express our thoughts and feelings to others while depressed and grieving. Below is a letter I wrote that might help you with both. I encourage you to share some form of this letter with your friends and family. It tries to explain the hurt and pain we are going through while asking our friends and family members to continue to be there when we need them the most.

Dear Friend or Family member,

Please be patient and understanding with me; I need to grieve in my own way and in my own time. Please do not try taking away my grief or fixing my pain. It would help me most if you just listened to me and let me cry on your shoulder. If you feel like it, please cry with me. Please forgive me if I say something stupid or insensitive. I always feel tired and exhausted and have very little left to give. Please let me express my feelings and talk about my memories. I encourage you to share your stories of Jenelle, Amy, and mom with me. I need to hear them. Please avoid telling me what to do or when to quit grieving. I get so tired of hearing clichés about grieving. Please do not ever tell me that "time heals all wounds", "they are in a better place", or "it was meant to be". These things are both hurtful and insensitive.

Nothing you can say to me will take away my pain. What I need are hugs, not words. Please do not push me to do things I am not ready to do or feel hurt if I seem withdrawn. This is a necessary part of my recovery.

Please never stop calling me. You might think you are respecting my privacy, but to me it feels like abandonment.

I will never be the same person as I was before. I have been through a traumatic experience, and I am a different person. **Please accept me for who I am today.**

Randy

Chapter 5

Different Behaviors Caused by Grief
I miss them so much!

- **Changed Behaviors.** A grieving person may struggle to fall asleep or stay asleep. He or she may also lose energy for enjoyable activities. The person may lose interest in eating or being social. A grieving person may also become more irritable or aggressive. Other common behaviors include restlessness and excessive activity.
- **Fatigue or Exhaustion.** This is the feeling of being extremely tired all the time and is one of the common early signs of grief that may keep you from getting out of bed each morning to accomplish daily tasks. Grief makes you tired because it is such an overwhelming emotion. Any time you deal with stressful and complex issues, such as grief, you will most likely be left emotionally and physically exhausted.
- **Dreams.** Could be good or bad. I pray every night for God to let me see Jenelle and Amy in my dreams. When it happens, it is a GREAT night. Sometimes when I close my eyes, I can picture them being in the accident or in their caskets during the visitation. Even though the bad dreams are terrible, I will suffer through them anytime just to see the girls in a good dream.
- **Sightings or seeing things.** This behavior really affected me. At numerous times, I would see teenage girls that looked like Jenelle. My confused mind would think it was her. Of course, I was always disappointed. I also remember several times when three deer were

playing together, and I thought it was Mom and the girls enjoying the day. These were positive sightings for me, and they reminded me of my family.

- **Sleeplessness.** Sleep is supposed to be when the body and brain rest and try to repair themselves. Sleep during grief can be disrupted via bad dreams, extra worries and stressors that have been caused by a recent loss, or the anxiety caused by those bad dreams. In short, grief and sleep loss create a vicious cycle where grief causes sleep problems, and those sleep problems can make the grief worse. If you are having sleep issues, your brain and body do not have that opportunity to fix themselves. This can be extremely frustrating for those who are grieving as it can be demoralizing to feel sad, anxious, and exhausted all at the same time.

Those first few weeks after the accident, I really struggled to fall asleep. I would lay down and close my eyes, and vivid pictures of the accident would portray in my mind. Even though I was just imagining what had happened, I emotionally felt what I thought Mom, Jenelle, and Amy went through during their last few seconds of life.

I reached out to my doctor for some sleep medicine. I realized that if I was not sleeping well or at all, the grief and pain I was feeling would start to compound. Besides the sleep medicine, we tried to make sure the bedroom was cool and dark. We also tried to stick to a regular time routine, and practiced relaxation techniques before going to bed.

- **Social Withdrawal.** Many grievers feel that they are a burden to their family and friends and do not reach out for their help. Instead of thinking "I need help", they are thinking that their family and friends already have lives, jobs, and their own problems and they do not want to burden them with their own grief. I am not saying this is right, but it does happen.

As a griever, you must make some tough decisions. You can decide to be very isolated from the public and grieve alone. On the other hand, you can decide that your loved ones would have wanted you to continue to live your life the best that you can and slowly return to the activities and functions that made you happy prior to their death. Char realized Jean, Jenelle and Amy had died and they would want her to live life to the fullest and not waste her life grieving forever for them. Char wrote a goodbye letter to Jenelle and Amy. This helped her to put aside her fantasies of them returning and really let them go. Many tears were involved, but they were good tears. It was time to start living life again for Randy and Matt's sake as well as her own.

- **Crying**. It is OK to cry. If somebody thinks you are weak because you are crying, that is his or her problem, not yours. A good friend of mine told me that crying does not wear a person out; it just makes them more miserable. I agree. Crying is a normal and natural grief reaction for most people who have experienced losing a loved one. Crying helps with the release of grief and sorrow. When you hold back tears, it registers stress in your brain and signals that something is wrong. If you feel like crying, CRY. A friend of ours who suffered a tragic loss suggested limiting the amount of time you cry each day. Instead of crying for several hours, she decided to cry for only 45 minutes at a time. She continued only allowing herself to cry a little less each day. This worked for her. It may not work for everyone.

I was the crier in my family, and still am. The stressful emotions brought about due to loss need to be released. I do not know why, but I always felt better after a few tears.

Dr. Alejandra Vasquez, JD, CT

Role:
Certified Grief Counselor
Expertise:
Death and bereavement, spiritual grief counseling, continuing bonds therapy
Education:
University of Central Florida, Bachelor of Arts in Political Science Florida Coastal School of Law, JD Association for Death Education and Counseling, Certification in Thanatology

Dr. Alejandra Vasquez wrote the article below that attempts to justify why we cry when we lose someone close to us.

Why Do We Cry When Someone Close to Us Dies?

Grief is a natural human experience, and crying is the ultimate healer. We cry at the death of those we know and love as an expression of our grief. Tears can transform suffering and help us pick up the pieces to move forward in our sadness. Whether you are supporting someone bereaved or going through it yourself, you will find that having a good cry can make you and everyone who is suffering feel better.

Sadness following a loved one's death affects everyone differently, and not everyone will cry after someone close to him or her dies. Your emotional responses are unique only to you. Whether you shed tears will depend on many factors that include past unresolved trauma that you may still be working through, or a general inability to show emotions.

Crying is part of the stages of grief and can be a healthy emotional release. We tear up for various reasons when we suffer losses, and most people report feeling better after they have had a good cry.

The following are some of the reasons why we cry when we lose someone close to us:

1. To release grief and sorrow
Crying is a normal and natural grief reaction for most people who have experienced losing a loved one. Crying can be the ultimate healer in the release of grief and sorrow.

When you hold back tears, it registers stress in your brain and signals that something's wrong. Allowing yourself to shed tears can be the emotional and physical release that your body needs. A good healthy cry from time to time will not only make you feel better but will help you move forward in your healing.

2. To feel better
When you allow your tears to flow freely and naturally, it will make you feel better to cry whenever the mood strikes. Crying releases specific mood enhancers that can instantly work to lift your mood when you are feeling overwhelmed with grief. It is also okay if you do not feel like crying.

Allow your feelings and emotions to flow freely without overthinking it. This can mean crying whenever you feel like it, as well as not forcing yourself to cry in front of others because they are expecting you to. You do not need to force tears to show others how sad you are over your loved one's death.

3. To cleanse
Crying helps to cleanse you from your pain and sorrow and begins the healing process. Having a crying spell is usually a good sign, especially for someone who is deeply depressed. Depression can have the effect of numbing your feelings and emotions.

Some people affected by sorrow are not able to cry when someone they know, and love dies. While crying can be a sign of depression, it can also be a way out of depression.

4. As a grief ritual
Crying at a funeral is a normal part of many cultures' traditions to express lamentation and regret the person's death. It is also a sign of respect and honor.

Some cultures practice what is referred to as a death wail? It's a mourning lament performed ritually soon after the death of a family member. A death wail is often performed at the funeral or wake. Not crying may be seen as a sign of disrespect.

5. Physical healing of pain and sorrow
Bottling up your tears creates a blockage of releasing emotions that help you heal from your pain and suffering. When you are feeling overwhelming grief, it helps to let go of your tears instead of fighting against them.

There is nothing wrong with crying after the death of a loved one. You cry because you love and miss them. Not crying can seem like an unnatural reaction to their death. However, do not feel guilty when the tears do not come right away or at all. You may be numb for a few weeks as you get over the initial shock of their death. Do not punish yourself if you are not yet ready to cry.

6. To seek support
There is comfort in shedding tears over the loss of a loved one. Crying can be a call to your friends and family to rally around you for comfort and support. They may not know how to comfort someone who is upset, but their collective effort can make a big difference in your healing process. In some ways, it is good to know that there is always someone there for you when you need emotional uplifting and support.

Chapter 6

Physical symptoms and effects of grief
She is denying, I am crying

- **Physical sensations.** Grief can cause physical sensations that may include tightness or heaviness in the chest or throat, nausea or an upset stomach, dizziness, headaches, physical numbness, muscle weakness or tension, and fatigue. We went through all of these sensations during our grief. Often, many of them at the same time.

Grief may also make you vulnerable to illness. Some health problems that could result include:

- **Digestive system issues.** Sometimes we seek or over seek food to combat our stressful periods of depression. Unfortunately, overeating during stressful periods can cause a nauseous feeling which can lead to multiple health concerns like binge eating, nausea, a total loss of appetite, or even IBS—irritable bowel syndrome. Just knowing that these symptoms could be a result of grief should help you to look out for them to help prevent them from happening. The combination of stress, nervousness, and the lack of eating caused Char and I lots of issues shortly after the accident. Our son, Matt, kept encouraging us to eat to stay strong and healthy.
- **Body Aches and pains** are common physical symptoms of grief. The additional stress hormones released during the grieving process stun the muscles in the body and can cause pain. Others

have told me that grief caused them back pain, headaches, and stiffness in their joints. Sometimes it is difficult to distinguish the difference between health issues caused by grief versus health issues caused by other illnesses.

- **Immunity issues**. Immense stress can make people more susceptible to catching colds and the flu.
- **Broken heart syndrome**—unbelievably, there are studies that show intense stress caused by grief can lead to heart risks including "broken heart syndrome". This is a disruption in the blood pumping to one section of the heart and causes both shortness of breath and chest pain. Over the years, I had to go through multiple stress tests just to make sure I was not having an actual heart attack. I had no idea there was a disease with the name "Broken Heart Syndrome". It makes sense because we suffered from this for years.
- **Self-harming behavior**—not eating or overeating are both unhealthy coping mechanisms. Others might turn to alcohol, drugs, or cigarettes. These high-risk behaviors can lead to long-lasting effects on your body.

I remember trying to "drown my sorrows" after Jenelle and Amy died. Unfortunately, the pain of loss supersedes any other types of pain like hangovers. I was never much of a "bar hopper", so I tried to see how much beer it took to forget about all my pain and sorrows. I determined that no amount of alcohol could override the pain caused by losing someone close to you. After a few days of heavy drinking, I decided that the headaches I would wake up with every morning were detrimental to my health.

Chapter 7

Thoughts and Beliefs of Grievers

Grieving really messes with your mind as well as with reality. Below are a few of the perception problems I suffered.

- Hallucinations can happen frequently when you are in the acute stage of grief. Both seeing things and hearing things about your loved one can be a normal reaction to bereavement. Sometimes grievers are too scared to share these thoughts with others because they fear them being seen as mentally unstable. I was trying to work a full-time job and run a business shortly after the accident. I was scared to death to share my fantasies and delusions with others. As a businessperson, I needed people to be able to rely on me. Most of this "pressure to perform" was self-driven. However, I still believe that others fully expect you to continue as before, even though you are still grieving.

Seeing or touching things that belonged to the girls would put me into that hallucinogenic stage. Char and I would often see other children with similar appearance to Jenelle and Amy. We would briefly get our hopes up that our daughters were still alive. We also hung onto some of their special blankets, clothing, and books. When we touch or see these memorable items, the memories come alive again.

My worst delusion is when I am over-tired and trying to get to sleep. I ask God to let me see my daughters' right before I go to bed. Sometimes he does, sometimes he does not. It is on these nights where my mind magically takes me to the site of where the accident occurred. I can see the girls having fun in the car with Grandma Jean right before their lives ended.

Do these hallucinations ever end? So far, after eighteen years, my answer would be NO. Do they get better and less intense? Yes, they do.

- Concern about the future (or lack of future)

Jenelle wanted to be an architect and design amazing homes and buildings. She could picture these properties via her creative imagination. Char and I were so excited about her future. My cousin, David, owned a large architectural firm in Dallas. They had discussed the possibility of Jenelle doing an internship at his firm and possibly even working there after her college graduation. Because of her early death, the world will never know the amazing homes and buildings she would have created.

Amy was only nine years old when she died. Her future was undecided, but still very promising. Through her leadership, she had created such a love of life that others emulated her.

On March 23, 2003, shortly before their death, nine-year old Amy wrote the following letter to Jenelle. It showed how close they were as sisters.

Dear Jenelle,

Jenelle, I am writing this letter to tell you how much I appreciate and love you. I appreciate for everything you do. You help me with projects and take me to special places. For instance, you take me to the mall and you even take me to plays. I really really appreciate that. It is very kind of you. I love so much, but I especially love you. Your kind and generous and hey your my sister. What else is there to love? Your so cool and very very pretty. Again, what is there to love more than a pretty, kind, generous, wonderful sister. I just wanted to let you know. Love you. Hugs and Kisses.

Yours truly,
Amy Stocker

Reading this letter helps me to feel better. It is nice to know that these two amazing sisters, who love each other so much, are together in heaven. I often tell people who lose children that Jenelle, Amy, and Grandma Jean will meet them at the door to heaven and welcome them to their new home. As you are comforting your friends and family who are grieving from tragic loss, be sure to mention that others will be waiting for them in heaven. I even think that maybe God needed all three of them in heaven at the same time to be on his "welcoming committee".

Just before she died, Amy's babysitter, Jill Shoot, shared the following story.

"As I was applying lipstick one day, Amy told me that the outside does not matter. "It is not the look that counts". She then reminded me to look at a person on the inside. If I can remember that, and maybe if we all could, the world would be much kinder and more accepting of each other. Jill stated, "Amy held so much potential. She was like a rose before it bloomed, tightly wrapped, and waiting for the right time to unfold and expose the beauty from within. Amy had just begun to bloom and to show the world her true beauty when her life was cut short, so no one will ever see or know her full beauty".

- **Confusion**—we were so confused immediately after we heard the news. It was difficult to concentrate and make decisions. The number of things that must happen immediately after learning of a sudden death are overwhelming. It was hard to remember what people were saying or suggesting that we do. It was like short-term amnesia.

- **Mind Concerns or Pre-Occupation**—the mind of a griever causes a tendency to repeat or go-over the events and details of the death. It can cause complete exhaustion, which can lead to other health issues.

I am writing this book eighteen years after Mom, Jenelle, and Amy died. I can still close my eyes and picture exactly what happened that day. I can see pictures of the remains of the car they were driving. Sometimes, I even imagine what it was like for them the final few seconds before they died. My brother, Gary, has shared that he frequently tries to imagine those few seconds before the crash and wonders if Mom, Jenelle, or Amy even had time to comprehend their fate. Many of us wrote notes to the truck driver, reminding him of how his actions that day took three lives and changed the lives of numerous other people–forever.

- **Disbelief**—this was the first thing that hit us. Char had just spoken to Jenelle and Amy a few hours before and they were fine. We thought the coroner was wrong or had made a mistake. No way could this have happened to us. This only happens to the "other guy".

We were starting to realize that something terrible had happened. Between the county coroner's being at our house, the coroner at the accident, and the phone call with Dad, our disbelief was slowly starting to change to "could this have really happened?" We prayed to God to ask him to make sure this was just a terrible misunderstanding.

Most people probably think this way, especially with sudden death. It is like a bad dream that came true. I kept waiting for someone to wake me up and tell me I was dreaming.

Chapter 8

Common routine changes for Grievers
Do not ever forget my child

After the death of a family member or close friend, you may notice many changes in your life. These could include:

- **A change in daily routine.** If you are used to spending time with a loved one, it can be quite a change in your daily habits when they pass. In our case, we were used to taking Amy to school every day and attending her soccer matches in the evenings. We had happily dedicated many hours each day to being part of her life. When she passed, we struggled to fill that missing time and create a new routine. We were her family and caregiver for nine amazingly short years. We felt lost by not having anybody to provide those caregiving responsibilities after her death.

  In Jenelle's case, we had a set 3:00 call time every Saturday while she was at college. Absolutely nothing got in the way of this weekly event as we anxiously awaited to learn more about her week at college. We greatly missed these much-anticipated calls.

  If you are attempting to help your grieving friend, try to keep in mind how his or her life has changed. Consider working with them to help create or develop a new routine. Unfortunately, something that disappears during times of uncertainty is an established routine. When grieving, it helps to stick to a familiar routine. This will help you to keep an element of normalcy in your life, as there are many positives in keeping with a balanced system. At times, we feel overwhelmed and out of control. An established routine can help us to feel better grounded and possibly help to restore a sense of normalcy to our lives. A structured lifestyle can help you to reduce the confusion and unhappiness you are facing.

Although it is important to stick to a familiar pattern or routine, do not try to overdo and set unachievable goals. Be sure to include some time to relax and some time to grieve. I read a book back in 2006 that encouraged grievers to "set aside" time to do your grieving each day. I tried this and found it to be very helpful in my situation. I blocked off between 3:00-4:00 pm each day, just to grieve. This allowed me to function more easily during the day. It also gave me something to look forward to each day–a full hour of yelling and screaming and maybe even some swearing. I wore myself out during this time and was better able to perform the rest of the day.

Some days of grieving will always be harder than other days. I found that the days leading up to special days like Father's Day or Thanksgiving or Christmas were the hardest for me. Instead of keeping my structured routine, I blocked off even more time during these "unusually tough days".

Jenelle, Matt, and Amy with proud papa at Christmas.

- **A change in relationships.** Not everybody is able to continue a similar relationship after the death of a loved one. Some family or friends simply may not know what to do or say around you. They might act different, say dumb things, or even distance themselves from you. They are not trying to hurt you; they just do not have the skills or perspective to be comfortable around you.

On the other hand, some may become closer to you because your lifestyle or interests might have changed. Thus, you might lose connections with some people while starting new relationships and friendships with others.

After our loss, we were able to reach out to others who had lost children or family members. Most of the time, people cannot honestly say "I know how you feel". However, we were able to say this to others who had suffered similar loss. Many of these people came to be some of our best friends.

Empathy means to put yourself in someone else's shoes. If you have not experienced the loss of a child or other loved one, empathy is almost impossible. Think about a parent who has lost a child to a chronic disease. Can anyone who has not experienced that have any idea what it is like to be in the proverbial shoes of those parents? "I know how you feel" is an absolute "no-no" when speaking with someone who has experienced such a loss.

Ask Yourself–How do I handle?

- **A change in financial or employment status**—when a spouse or partner dies, you may have to assume some of the duties they previously handled. Tasks like paying the bills or handling the insurance may be completely unfamiliar to you. Learning new things while grieving adds a ton of stress to the griever. If that person was also the main wage earner, you may need to get a job or work more hours, just to make ends meet

I was very fortunate to work for a family owned company called Dot Foods. The Tracy family stepped right up and told me not to worry about money issues and job concerns. They offered to help in any way possible including financially. There was absolutely no pressure to return to work. Although we did not need their money, it was extremely comforting to know that it was available. Thank you to the Tracy family for everything you did after this accident. You took the pressure off having to make tough money decisions at a time when I was not thinking very clearly.

If you are a manager of people, I encourage you to take the same approach the Tracy family took for me. Show patience, offer to help, or assist whenever needed, and be proactive with your employees by anticipating their needs. Do not say, "Call me if you need anything". Instead, it is important that you understand the amount of stress, pain, and suffering the griever is going through and be patient with them.

When Jenelle died, she had a substantial college loan with Drury University. We did not know if we should continue to pay the loan or not. Fortunately, somebody encouraged us to reach out to the bank and explain our situation. We did so and the bank was able to waive the remainder of her college loan.

Sometimes, the breadwinner may be the person that died. In that case, the loss of income could be substantial and could lead to major hardships like homelessness or mal-nourishment due to lack of money to buy food.

As a good friend:

1. Try to understand what financial questions or assistance your friend might need. Then, help them to do the research and provide suggestions or options. Remember; do not ever tell somebody who is grieving what to do.
2. Try to understand that "secondary losses" can sometimes be extremely important to the survivors. Try to find out what those losses might entail —and try to help resolve them. If having enough money to buy groceries is an issue, put them in touch with a food pantry or ask for private donations to help.

- **A change in your Faith—** After the death of someone you love, you may question your religious or spiritual beliefs or your understanding of the meaning of life. On the other hand, you may find that your faith becomes stronger and a source of comfort.

Char and I were the exact opposite when it came to God. I was more into blaming God for not protecting my daughters. I kept asking myself "why was I being punished?" I went to mass regularly, but often got so upset during the church service that I would leave and go to the cemetery to be with Jenelle and Amy. Char probably spent more time at church those first few months after the accident because she felt better in the presence of the Lord.

- **A change in your priorities**—Most of us need to fill the void in our daily lives with something different. Your priorities and goals could change to reflect your new lifestyle without your loved one.

We struggled to get out of bed each morning. For a while, that was our daily goal. If we could get out of bed, eat some breakfast, and then go to work, we would have achieved our objective for that day.

As time went on, we became more protective of our son, Matt. He was all we had left. It was not fair to him to have Mom and Dad watching him all the time. However, protecting him from everything was a priority. Once you have lost a loved one, you do anything humanly possible to protect your other loved ones.

It was about six months after the accident when Char mentioned adoption. We had joined Big Brother/Big Sister for a while and spent time with a beautiful young woman, Sarah, who needed some extra support and love. We realized after working with her, that we were not ready to be empty nesters. We were still caregivers and still had a lot of love to share. Although Char was ready to either adopt or have another child, I just was not sure that I wanted to start over again. We were also getting older—she was 47 and I was 45 years old. Having another child was not physically possible for us.

We agreed to start the adoption process and chose to adopt a beautiful little girl from China. It took about 23 months to complete the process, but on December 25, 2005, in Guangzhou, China, we were introduced to our new daughter, Melissa Mei. Our lives had changed once again as we now had another child to love and nurture.

Above is a picture of Melissa and me when we arrived back in the United States, shortly after the adoption. The second picture is of Melissa graduating from Lourdes High School in Rochester, MN. From left to right, Matt, Char, Melissa, and me. Two amazing days in the history of my family.

She has been a big part of our lives since that day and has helped us survive the loss of Jenelle and Amy. Melissa is now attending college at Drake University and plans to be a pharmacist when she graduates.

Chapter 9

Everybody Grieves Differently

Ten Things we did
Or
How many times can you hit a punching bag?

Everybody grieves differently—below are ten things that we did to help us get through those long, miserable days. Some may sound silly, but they all helped.

1. My Punching Bag—when grieving, it is important to have some type of outlet for your anger. Daily, I would get so angry and mad at the world that I needed a way to release my frustrations. I would go downstairs and take it out on a punching bag. Believe me when I say that I had lots of anger. I kept this yellow bag in the basement and would just hit and kick the bag while screaming at the top of my lungs—**I miss my daughters.** My son, Matt, would get so worried that he would call a good friend to check on me. I truly hated worrying my son, but just being able to take out my anger helped me get through the day.

2. Antidepressants—I never thought that I would ever take depression medicine. I was wrong. During my grief, I could feel the pain growing within me. It would get to a point where I felt I was about to explode. I erupted frequently those first several months. Finally, my doctor convinced me to start taking an antidepressant medication. I did have some issues with insomnia and nausea at first. My dreams were also much more intense than they had been in the past. I am a man—men are strong—but GRIEF IS STRONGER. It took a few weeks for this medicine to start helping, but when it did, the medicine helped to level my emotions out so I was able to function better.

Char was already taking some medicine prior to the girl's death. She was more levelheaded and less moody than I was at first, probably because she was already taking antidepressants.

One thing I learned about depression medicine—do not stop taking it. I do not know how they do it, but the antidepressants kept my mood and emotions balanced. It was a good feeling to have less emotional upheaval each day. I tried going cold turkey three different times over the first few years. That emotional balance disappeared quickly, and I went into a deep depression all three times. I was not suicidal, but everything that triggered my grief—seemed to be amplified when I was not on my depression medicine. I am sure that most people react differently to this type of medication. As you are keeping an eye on your friends that are grieving, encourage them to inform you if they attempt to quit taking their medicine, as you will need to keep a much closer eye on them when they do.

It is now eighteen years after Jenelle and Amy and Mom died. I still take depression medicine. To this day, if I forget to take it for even a couple of days, my mind and body go back into that deep feeling of hopelessness and despair. It is not as bad as it was eighteen years ago, but it still affects my life.

3. Exercise until it wears you out. Our good friend Becky shared this one with me. She was unable to sleep after her husband died back in 2003. She chose to join an exercise group in Quincy. Her purpose was to get to know the other widows in the group while physically wearing herself out so she could sleep at night. Besides this exercise group, Becky and Char did a lot of bicycling and took long walks. Anything to wear them out and allow them to sleep better.

4. Frank Sinatra at the cemetery—actually, it was me, Randy Stocker at the cemetery singing to Jenelle and Amy. We used to all sing songs together on road trips. I guess that I was pretending that they were still with me when we were singing. One of our favorites was "One Tin Soldier" by The Original Caste. The song is about a kingdom on a mountain and the valley folk below. The valley folk wanted the treasure buried deep beneath the stone. The mountain people offered to share this treasure, but the valley people decided they wanted it all for their own. When the valley folk finally reached the treasure, a stone said, **"PEACE ON EARTH."**

This song talks about what is most important to people. The girls really liked it because it talked about "Peace on Earth" and that was important to them.

5. Reverse birthday parties for the friends of Amy and Jenelle. This was totally Char's idea. We had a birthday party for Amy at the cemetery and invited her friends and teachers. We turned it around by giving gifts from Amy to each of her friends that attended. This party helped us to remember how Amy was such a kindhearted and giving person. Even from the grave, she was able to make her friends happy by providing those gifts.

6. Balloon Releases—we helped organize several balloon releases over the years. The concept is simple and means a lot to the families of those that are deceased. We bought a bunch of helium balloons and invited anybody that had suffered a tragic loss and wanted to remember their loved ones in a unique way. We picked out a location—usually a church parking lot or a cemetery. We asked that each person use a magic marker to write a message to his or her loved ones. At the appointed time, we all released our helium balloons. Seeing hundreds of balloons rising into the air at the same time heading toward those in heaven that we missed and loved was a beautiful sight. It was a different way to both bring people together and to provide a unique way for them to send a message to their loved ones. Try it. We have also done this a few times just by ourselves.

7. Around the Table—my family, including aunts and uncles and cousins met at a hotel in Bloomington, IL in 2018. The last day we were all sitting around, and somebody suggested that everybody share stories about either mom, Jenelle, or Amy. It was so neat to hear some of these stories—some that we had never heard before. You do not have to be in a large group to make something like this an effective tool to help those that are grieving. The next time a bunch of family and friends are together—just suggest going "around the table" and share stories about your loved ones.

We did something similar when Char's brother and father passed away. We used to play cards (poker) with them frequently. After they passed, we started to include them in the last poker hand that we played. We all added some money to the pot, and then we dealt everybody five cards, including Mikel and Mack. If they won the best hand, we would donate their winnings to the church. Most of the time we cheated and played until either Mack or Mike won the pot. It was more fun that way. This event always got us smiling and telling more stories about them.

8. My Two Little Angels—one of the nicest gifts I received after the girls died came from a good friend that I worked with. We had worked together for several years. She had lost a child even before Jenelle and Amy died in their tragic accident. She gave me two little silver angels to always carry with me. These silver angels helped me get through several tough days. I carried these angels for years and would pull them out of my pocket whenever I was feeling down. Most people talk about angels keeping an eye on you—I just carried mine in my pocket with me. Eighteen years later, I still carry them. The negative of doing this is that sometimes they get misplaced. Unfortunately, it still hurts whenever I lose them because it feels like I was losing my girls all over again.

Consider giving your grieving friends the type of gift that helps them to remember that their loved ones are always with them. These little angels sure made an impact on me—and it might make a positive impact on your friends as well.

We received many other meaningful gifts including:

- An angel water fountain. Some of my friends at Dot Foods gave us this beautiful fountain. The soothing flow of water helped us to de-stress and relax.
- A tree to help keep our memories alive. Our friends, Brad and Becky, gave us a tree to plant in honor of Jenelle and Amy. Looking at this tree over the years helped us to keep a piece of their memory alive while we moved forward with our lives. When we moved to Minnesota, we got permission to re-plant this tree at the Quincy cemetery close to the girls. Every time we visit our daughters at the cemetery in Quincy, we think about this wonderful gift.
- Comfort or service gifts like pre-paid gift cards at our favorite restaurants.
- Tribute gifts like photos, engraved objects, or donations in the memory of the girls all meant so much to us. Friends, family, and people we did not even know donated money towards the scholarships that were set up to honor the lives of Jenelle and Amy.

Unfortunately, most people do what is easy and send flowers or bring food to help comfort those who suffered the loss. These are both important but are more "short-term" gifts. If you want your gift to be more memorable, think of something that will remind the griever about their loved one for many years to come.

9. Counseling and Grief Groups—attending counseling and grief groups had both positive and negative effects on us. There are both good and bad reasons to use counselors and attend grief groups. First, most counselors are speaking to you about what they learned in a class or from a book. It is my thought that no matter how many books you read and/or conferences you attend; you just cannot understand the harshness of grief on a person. I sat with a few counselors and listened to their talks—all the while I was thinking to myself—have you had two daughters and a Mom killed at one time? Have you ever had to plan two funerals and two visitations within one week? Do you know what it feels like to outlive your nine-year-old?

Sure, the charts, graphs, and ways to grieve serve a purpose and I did learn about what was to come from some of this information. What I really needed was for somebody to sit down with me that had a similar loss to mine-and simply listen to me and answer my questions. We did not have that option back in 2003.

Because there were not any bereavement groups at our church, we decided to help form one. I feel that most communities need some type of well-promoted grief and bereavement program. The purpose of our group was to share what we learned with each other. It just helped so much to have somebody to talk to who was grieving just like me.

10. The importance of Memorials—one of the best things we did after the girls died was to ask our friends to write stories about Jenelle, Amy, and Mom. We received over 100 stories from friends, family members, and total strangers. We created a memory book that we shared with family and friends.

We had this picture taken shortly after their death. The photographer did a great job of adding the most recent pictures of Jenelle and Amy to our photo. I keep updating Melissa's picture and adding it to the photo. Although we are not all together, we are still a strong family.

We read these memorials on a regular basis. A few paragraphs that really touched our hearts include the following:

From Amy Beck. A good friend of the family.

"As for Amy, the Beck family, and especially the little Beck girls, looked up to Amy Stocker. They never just called her Amy. It is always "Amy Stocker. It made us think of presidents or famous people: those too important for just a first name like George Bush, Tom Cruise, or Michael Jordan". **Can Amy Stocker come over? Amy Stocker gave that to me. But Amy Stocker says."**

We affectionately referred to Amy Stocker as the neighborhood drill sergeant. Countless times you could look between our backyards and see Amy with all the neighborhood children, like a mother duck with her ducklings. She organized the games, which usually included obstacle courses, races, secret passwords, whistles to start and stop the action and the most important part to our girls —Prizes! Amy would bring prizes from her own room to give the girls when they won or at least tried their best. We have so many of Amy's prizes around our home that it reminds us of her daily."

"We are thankful for the positive example Amy set for our girls. She was extremely polite and when she left our home, I felt the need to work harder on manners with my own children. I remember the first time Amy came over for breakfast before school. The only cereal I had that she liked was Fruit Loops and it was down to the last few crumbs with maybe four loops. I poured the powdered cereal in her bowl, and she said "May I have a spoon please? She then proceeded to eat both bites before telling me, thank you that was delicious. This is just one example of the character she exhibited daily."

I remember my last earthly encounter with Amy. We were at College for Kids, and I was accompanying my Abby to her last day of class. I had recently had baby Clare, so I was also lugging our newest edition, along with the gear it takes for a newborn. I met Amy as we entered the building and she immediately took my diaper bag, freeing up an arm. She began to carry it to class for me until I mentioned that I was in search of my morning coffee. She then made sure Abby got to her class, pointed Char to her classroom, and then began taking me to the cafeteria to find coffee. The store area was closed, but she did not give up yet. She asked a small class in session when the cafeteria store opened and with no answers, she took me back to the vending machine area. Amy Stocker was very much a take-charge girl.

From Jill Shoot: A good friend of the family and Amy's babysitter.

"The week before Amy's life was taken; she came to a vacation Bible school with our family. The week focused on shining God's light to others. Amy loved the music and when she sang, it came from her heart. Amy was a true light who shined brightly and will continue to shine in our hearts forever. She is so dearly missed. That a young child was taken does not make any sense to us, and it never will here on earth. Amy's life was so short, but what an impression that precious child left upon everyone who met her. I can only hope to live life to the fullest like Amy did".

From Jan Faler: A family friend from church wrote the following about Jenelle:

"On Sunday, July 20, (two days before she was killed), sweet Jenelle came up to me and said, I just wanted to tell you that I love the way you accessorized your

dress today. *I just love that pin. We both agreed that we loved bright, happy colors and this orange flower pin with red centers was just that. Then we had a nice little chat about how it is a good idea to buy things that last and that this pin was made when I was Jenelle's age. We gave each other a hug and I just had such a warm, nice feeling that this young girl would bother to take the time and compliment me".*

Stories like these allowed us to remember how Jenelle and Amy lived their lives and how they were able to affect others here on earth. I have mentioned how important it is to share stories about the deceased person. If you can put them in writing and share them with their loved ones, it is better yet. As I am writing this section of the book, tears are just pouring down my face as I remember Jenelle and Amy. To those who shared these beautiful stories about our family, we thank you.

Best buddies. Jenelle and Amy always had a blast together. Talk about the perfect "big sister", Jenelle was it.

Pets and Grieving–How pets help you to survive grief

Right before she died, Amy and I picked out a brand-new pet for our house. It was a cat that she named "Tiger". She absolutely loved Tiger and spent much of her free time either chasing the cat or dressing it up. Tiger was very important to her.

After the accident, Tiger provided us with lots of companionship as well as emotional support. The cat knew that something was wrong, and someone was missing. I truly believe that Tiger grieved for Amy.

Char, Matt, and I felt that Tiger helped us through our emotional rollercoaster for those first few years. Where else can you receive both undivided attention and love other than from a pet?

You may or may not have any pets, but keep in mind that they can provide help and love and support during those dark times of grief. Some of the benefits we noticed included:

- Tiger forced us to be active. We were not able to lay around all day when we knew that we had to feed our cat and help it to exercise. Exercise is good for a griever as it creates something within us that positively affects our mood, sleep, and social behavior.
- Tiger comforted us. We felt so lost without Amy around. The cat provided a sense of both reassurance and comfort to us during those downtimes. We were able to share our feelings with our cat. He never talked back to us or told us what to do.
- Tiger gave us unconditional love. He was always there when we got home. He was always there when we were crying or angry. I have heard the term "furry therapists". I believe that Tiger served as our "furry therapist".

It was nice having Tiger around for nearly fifteen years after the girls were killed. He did not replace them, but he did remind us of better times when they were alive. When Tiger died in 2017, it probably hurt more than it should, because we felt like a piece of Amy died with him.

Chapter 10

Holidays and Grieving
Helping yourself

- Who is going to make the homemade noodles this year? Grandma always did it.
- Who will lead all the cousins in make-believe games and activities this year during the Memorial Day family gathering? Amy was always one of the leaders.
- I do not feel like celebrating Christmas this year without the girls.
- What are we supposed to do each year on the girl's birthdays?

There are so many special days and holidays that serve as a constant reminder of loss. Christmas and Thanksgiving were two of the hardest for my family. However, missed birthdays, Father's Day and Mother's Day, and Memorial Day were all hard. Families are all supposed to be together for these fun events.

Watching others celebrate and have fun can be both overwhelming and painful. These issues are probably the strongest during that first year after loss, but they are still present for many years to come.

Labor Day 2003 was probably the hardest day for me. Once a year for many years, my entire family got together at Mom and Dad's home in Gibson City. There were always ping-pong tournaments, swimming, and the very competitive wiffle ball game. All twenty-eight of us celebrated life as a family for this special event and looked forward to it for months prior.

The year (2003) was different. Despite the deaths of Mom, Jenelle, and Amy, we all still got together just a few months after the accident. Although everybody tried to make the best of it, this tragedy was on everybody's mind.

I remember when it was time to take the overall family picture. Something that we tried to do every year. I recall going crazy trying to understand why my brothers and sisters were even considering taking a family photo—when three members of the family died recently. In my opinion, we were not a family without Mom, Jenelle, and Amy. I remember being a real jerk and refusing to take part in the event. Fortunately, one of my brothers came up with the suggestion that we take the family portrait while holding 8X10 photos of the girls and Mom.

I share this story because grieving during the holidays can be very painful. The memories of previous family gatherings served as constant reminders of our loss.

We learned the following things to help get us through the holidays and other tough days. Thoughts include that:

- It is OK to grieve during the holidays but allow yourself the time to feel happiness as well as sadness and anger. Experiencing joy and laughter during a time of grief does not make you a bad person.
- It is important to set realistic expectations for yourself. If you do not feel like cooking or hosting an event, do not do it. Ask for help. Others are usually willing to step up, but sometimes you need to tell them what you need them to do.
- It is never good to isolate yourself by canceling the holiday. It is OK to avoid some issues that you do not feel comfortable with, but do not try to hide from all of them. Try to make some personal time for being by yourself. However, try to balance your solitude with some social activities that you enjoy.
- It is so important to take care of yourself. It is too easy to overeat or over drink to drown your sorrows in either food or alcohol. Keep an eye on yourself or ask a good friend or family member to keep

an eye on you. Sometimes a reminder from somebody important to you will keep you from heading in the wrong direction.

- It is OK to start new holiday traditions. That first Christmas after the accident, our good friends Brian and Mary Jo, invited us to their home for a Christmas Eve gathering. After some great food and conversation, we all attended Christmas Eve mass together. This tradition continued for ten years and helped us deal with the anxiety and sadness the holiday would inevitably bring.

- It is most important to remember that there is no right or wrong way to celebrate a holiday after the death of a loved one. Planning is the best way to cope. It is also important to ask for help and support from others and take it easy.

This is a picture of Jenelle celebrating her birthday. Holidays and parties were not the same without Jenelle and Amy.

Holidays and Grieving–Helping others

What type of help or assistance do grieving people want during the holidays? Below are my thoughts:

- Try proactively talking about the grief instead of ignoring it. It is scary for some people to be around the intense emotional roller coaster of a grieving person. Instead of pretending that nothing happened, it helped us when people would say things like "I know it is a tough time right now for you and your family. I am here for you if you simply want to talk. I am a good listener."

- Try being a GREAT listener. This does not mean giving advice or offering solutions to their problems. It means allowing the person to talk about their experience so you can fully understand their emotions. A good listener helps a grieving person feel heard, supported, and accepted. It also tells them that it is OK to talk openly about their loss.

- Try sharing some memories from previous holidays. My family was always great about sharing stories about Mom and the girls. Sometimes we laughed at the stories and sometimes they made us cry. However, we truly enjoyed hearing all the stories because they helped keep the memories alive.

- Try to understand that it is OK for a person to be sad during the holidays. We learned that it was better to be sad and let our grief out instead of trying to hold it in to make others feel more comfortable. Allow some time and space for them to feel sad or angry or to cry. Even in the middle of a party, if a griever feels like being alone, please encourage them to do so. I remember leaving family gatherings to go to a bedroom and cry. My family would always check on me, but they let me have my crying time. I read something that said, "Grieving doesn't dampen the holidays, rather, our reactions to grieving does". In summary, do not overreact when somebody leaves the party to be alone or cry for a while because that is what they need to do at that time.

- Try inviting grievers to every event that you would have invited them to if they were not grieving. Some people may not feel like doing anything because it might be a difficult time for them. That is OK. Respect their decisions if they decline your invitation. Be flexible and tell them that you understand and then invite them to the next function as well.

- Do not criticize how a griever is handling the holidays. If they do not want to decorate their home, that is OK. Sayings like "how about we brighten up this room by setting up a Christmas tree" could be looked at as unsolicited advice and being critical of the griever. The holidays are always hard enough; grievers do not need people judging and telling them they are not being festive enough.

Chapter 11

Coping with change
"I am really angry"

Below are several strategies or ideas that may help you better cope with the stressful changes that follow a loved one's death:

- **Take your time when making decisions.** The year after the death of a loved one is very emotional. Mental health experts strongly suggest waiting at least twelve months before making any major decisions.

Unfortunately, there are numerous decisions made immediately after a death. Decisions regarding visitations, funeral songs, flowers, and cemetery spots all need to happen sooner rather than later. Reach out to someone you trust to help provide help with these issues

We struggled with the decision-making process and the recommendations of the experts. Within one-year of the accident, we decided to adopt a new child, move to a new house and neighborhood, sell our business, and change careers.

Bad decision #1—We felt that we had good reasons for making all these decisions. First, it was so hard to remain in the house where Jenelle and Amy had lived with us. The memories were too strong in the home. Then again, we felt bad because we were moving away from the home where we had wonderful memories of Jenelle and Amy. We were hoping that moving to a new house would make it easier—it did not. The memories of a loved one will always be with you. It doesn't matter where you live.

Bad decision #2—I had frequently traveled when Jenelle and Amy were young and missed attending many of their events and activities. I told myself that I wanted to be a full-time father to Matt and our newly adopted daughter, Melissa. I never wanted to miss another one of my kid's activities—for the rest of my life. My new job allowed me to be home every night and help raise my children. I left a great company where I had worked for eighteen years. I could have and should have stayed at Dot Foods. Instead, I ended up working for eight different companies over the next fifteen years.

Bad decision #3—We had owned a Pak Mail franchise for five years. The business was growing and fun to own. After the accident, we chose to sell it to the first available buyer. We just could not handle the additional stress of owning and managing a business on top of our non-stop grieving. After a while, we realized that we should have kept this business. We enjoyed it and made some money running it.

Great Decision—our decision to adopt a child was by far the best decision that we have ever made. We went to China in mid-December 2005 and brought home a beautiful two-and-a-half-year-old daughter. We named her Melissa Mei. We were so happy and blessed to make her a part of our family. Our son, Matt, was able to go to China with us. Ever since the adoption, they have been very close siblings. She helped to provide some of the joy, laughter, and love that we had been missing since Jenelle and Amy died.

Before the adoption, I was scared that I would always be comparing Melissa to Jenelle and Amy. This was my grief talking, not me. Melissa is a unique and amazing child. It was a true blessing when she became part of our family.

This is Melissa shortly after we got her home from China. That beautiful smile on her face allowed me to be happy during a time when otherwise I was always sad. It was hard to be sad anytime Melissa was nearby.

- **Ask for and accept help.** Friends and family will want to help but might not know what you need or how to ask you if you need help. Be specific about your needs. Create a list of tasks that others can do. Make sure your friends understand that grief is never straightforward. You can show progress one day, and then fall back into your angry and frustrated self the next. If you are learning how to complete unfamiliar tasks, such as cooking or bill paying, ask someone to show you what to do. Overall, I think that people really want to help. They just do not know how.

- **Try keeping a journal.** Doing this can help you make sense of the changes that you are experiencing. In addition to writing about your feelings and thoughts, you can use your journal to help you organize tasks, priorities, and plans. Looking back through your journal can help you see how your priorities and goals have changed and how your ability to cope has improved. Your journal can also remind you of the hard times and what you did to get through them.

Char kept a journal for several years. She used it to write thoughts and letters to both Jenelle and Amy. She would remind them of things they used to do together. I think this journaling helped her to process her grief.

Below is a letter Char wrote to Jenelle on March 8, 2004

Jen, I am burning red candles today and all I see is your blood pouring out. This is how you would think! I miss you so damn much. I miss looking forward to celebrating our birthdays together. I miss your joy and enthusiasm. I miss your love, your hugs, your voice, your pep, and your sanity! I even miss your grumpy moods, which were far between, except in the morning when we were getting you up. I miss your weird way of dressing. I miss our road trips together. I miss your smile. New York was such a kick. I miss watching movies with you, the funny ones, and the weird ones. I miss your artistic talent and the way you always did things so differently. You put your heart and soul into everything you did. I miss your clumsiness; we were so alike in this respect. I like how you shared your faith as I did. I loved your determination, maybe even your stubbornness. I hated most of your music, but then we loved a lot of the same music as well—especially any retro music or music remakes.

Remember the Backstreet Boys concert that we went to. It was great! What a wonderful time together. What a friend you were to me. Fortunately, I was your mom, too. Wow, how awesome was that!

If it helps to put your thoughts in writing, please do so. If somebody thinks that you are silly for writing to the deceased, that is their problem, not yours. When grieving, do whatever feels right to you.

Instead of journaling, I went to the cemetery on a regular (sometimes-daily) basis and talked with Jenelle and Amy. I would share how much I missed them and how my life had changed without them as part of it. Whatever works best for you is what you need to do. Do not worry about what other people are thinking and saying.

Eighteen years later, I still talk with Jenelle and Amy on a regular basis. I share stories about what Melissa is doing at college and how proud we are to have her as part of the family. I talk about Matt, Sierra, and the grandsons and the joy and happiness they bring to us daily. I tell them what Char and I are doing and how much we miss them. It may sound silly, but talking to Jenelle and Amy–even eighteen years after they passed, helps me to get through a tough day.

- **Memorializing our loved ones**–Members of our grief support group shared several ways that ensured their loved ones will always be remembered forever. One of the things shared that we liked and did for our girls was a balloon release.
- **Remember the positive.** For a long time after their death, I was blaming God for taking the girls from me. After learning more about Free Will, I started thanking God for the nine and nineteen years he allowed me to be with Jenelle and Amy.

Chapter 12

Grief or Bereavement Support Groups
How they helped us

- **Consider joining a support group.** Support groups provide you the chance to talk with others who are going through similar experiences and who are experiencing similar feelings. They help participants cope with both emotions and stress while allowing members to bond together while sharing their individual experiences. Other people who have lost a loved one have most likely experienced many of the same changes that you have. They can offer you emotional support and practical advice as you adjust.

Instead of joining a support group, we formed one in Quincy, IL. We realized there was a lack of experienced help available to comfort and listen to those of us who were grieving. We named our group, "The Quincy Area Bereavement Group". We met on a regular basis with others who were grieving. We shared stories, cried together, and learned how to help each with our grief together. This group was very beneficial to Char and me. The benefit of sharing our story with others helped us to get through the day. If you do not have a group or organization in your town, consider starting one on your own. You might be surprised how many people are grieving and that would attend your meetings.

Four areas that helped us the most while participating in these groups including:

1. <u>Being able to tell our story</u>-the group allowed us to openly share our story with the rest of the attendees. We were able to explain the personal experiences of our loss in a shared format. It is much easier to "open up" when you are with others who are also grieving.

2. <u>Dealing with emotions</u>—we were able to share with the group how we handled or did not handle our emotions. The purpose was to see how others handled similar circumstances, and to learn from each other. We learned that many grievers simply give up and accept that they will be in grief for the rest of their lives. Our group taught each of us that to make our own personal decisions about whether to accept the death and move on with life or continue to let the deaths affect our lives in a negative way.

3. <u>Understanding more about secondary losses</u>—Those who are grieving usually have lost more than just a friend or family member. They have also lost the roles and functions of the person that died. Tasks like paying the bills, shoveling the snow, or hauling children around are still required. With Jenelle already in college and Amy only nine years old, we did not have many secondary losses. Ours was more the loss of fun and loving companionship from our daughters.

4. <u>Resolving outstanding situations and unfinished business</u>—Unanticipated issues seem to appear frequently after a loss. The griever needs to step up or take care of any outstanding situations left behind by the deceased. These can be both emotional and physically draining. We had already paid for Jenelle's second year at Drury University in Springfield, MO. We were not sure if we were even entitled to get her tuition refunded. Fortunately, after some help from a professor at her college, we were able to get our money back. This money helped us pay the bills involved in two funerals.

Chapter 13

Ways to Honor and Remember your Loved One

When we lose someone that we love, an important part of the grief journey is how we choose to reevaluate our relationship with that person. Our relationship and routines changed as we went through different times in our life. After the loss, we needed to decide if we should get away from doing old habits and traditions. Below are some things that we have done to help remember our loved ones.

- **Balloon Releases**—we helped to organize several balloon releases over the years. We purchased some helium balloons and black magic markers. We then wrote notes to Mom, Jenelle, and Amy on the balloons. Then, at a specific time, (ex. New Year's Eve at midnight) we let them go. It really felt like we were communicating with our loved ones in a different way. Sometimes we also organized large groups of people and let our balloons go all at the same time.

Note: Although balloon releases are popular, the balloons can be harmful to the environment and to wildlife.

- **Plant a tree in honor of someone who has died**. Visit it on special days and maybe even decorate it as you watch it grow.

Our good friends Brad and Becky gave us a tree after the girls passed. We planted it in our backyard and watched it grow. When we decided to move, we received permission from the local cemetery to plant the tree close to the girl's gravesite. This amazing gift keeps on living.

- **My Little Angels**—a friend I worked with gave me a gift of two tiny silver angels. I carried them for years as they reminded me of Jenelle and Amy. I misplaced them a few times over the years. It was amazing how not being able to find my "little angels" caused me additional anxiety and stress. It was like losing the girls again. Consider carrying something with you that will always remind you of your loss.
- **Create a new relationship with the deceased** Instead of detaching yourself from the deceased, try creating a new relationship. In other words, grief is ongoing. I had never heard about this theory, but simply started talking and singing to Jenelle and Amy the day they died. It was a way for me to keep the communication open with them. It helped bring back some normalcy during a tough time. Char began keeping a journal and writing to the girls frequently. She would write about how much she missed them, what her day was like, and how she was feeling that day. We were still both communicating with our daughters—just in different ways.
  - **Family gatherings**—create a gathering of friends and family to get together to share stories, memories, and pictures of your loved one. This is a way to honor them and help you as well.
    My family all got together in Bloomington, IL in 2018. On the last day there, the adults and older children took turns telling stories about Mom, Jenelle, and Amy. We had heard some of the stories before but heard several new ones as well. We did cry, but only because it was such an amazing gathering and so many different people shared stories about our loved ones.
  - **Closet cleaning**—it was very hard to throw away anything that belonged to Jenelle and Amy. Everything meant something to us, so it was overwhelming to do. Char asked one of her good friends to help sort through the clothes and mementos. Having a friend to talk to during this traumatic time was very helpful.
  - **Say their names**—you may not realize how much you miss hearing their name. Start saying it yourself and bringing it up to others. If they see that you are proactively talking about your

loved one, they will as well. Many people are scared to mention the name of a deceased person because they are uncomfortable saying it and worried that it might upset you. Take charge if you are comfortable. Others will follow your lead.

I asked others how important it is to hear the names of their loved ones who had passed and received the following responses:

- At first, it hurt too bad…almost seven years later it is comforting. Hugs… the heartbreak never goes away.
- I feel a sense of peace when I talk about family members that have passed. It might bring sadness, but it also brings joy that their memory carries on.
- Always brings a fond memory when I hear the name of a lost loved one.
- In the beginning, I did not want to talk about my late husband. It hurt so badly. As time passed, it helped me to talk to others about him. I wanted to keep him alive by talking about him.
- We love it when someone remembers our son. I think some family members are uncomfortable when we talk about him, but he will always be our little boy.

Honor their dream—was there something fun or exciting that your loved one always wanted to do? If so, think about a way to honor them by doing it.

Mom always wanted to take the whole family to Disney World in Florida. It was her dream. Dad and I decided to make the dream come true by taking 27 people—five kids, five spouses, dad, and sixteen grandchildren to Disney. We timed it around the one-year anniversary of the accident. We held a special ceremony in Florida for Mom and the girls. Although it was a sad event, it created so many memories for everybody that attended. Thanks again, Mom, for your dream.

Here is a picture of all twenty-seven of us in Florida.
It was a sad, but enjoyable trip for all.

People normally have fun while at Disney World. Unfortunately, while the younger children were enjoying the many activities of the theme park, the rest of us were struggling to keep it together. Gary reminded me of a story where he and I sat crying outside a Disney restaurant while others walked by in shock and discomfort. Most people probably figured out that something bad had happened but had no idea how bad.

While on this trip, we held an event on the one-year anniversary of the accident. We dedicated this trip to Mom, Jenelle, and Amy. We all shared stories of their amazing lives, cried about their unbelievable deaths, and just became a closer family.

- **<u>Reverse Birthday parties</u>**—Amy loved birthday parties and celebrating with her friends. Since Amy was only nine when she died, we decided to hold a birthday party at the cemetery on her tenth birthday. We used the chapel and invited many of her friends, their families, and Amy's teachers. Instead of her friends bringing gifts for Amy, we provided gifts for her friends. Amy was a very giving person. Through this birthday party, she was able to keep giving, even after her death. At Jenelle's 20th birthday, we gathered at the gravesite. Jenelle had been trying to learn to play the guitar before she died. Matt decided to take over and taught himself to play. His first real song was when he played the guitar and sang Happy Birthday during her birthday celebration. That was very touching.

<u>Set additional plates at your table</u>. If you are used to having five people at your dinner table, as we were, set more plates. We did this at both the Christmas and Thanksgiving holidays for several years. It helped us to remember the girls during the tough holiday seasons.

These are just ten of the things we did to help honor and remember Jenelle, Amy, and Mom. Other potential ideas include:

- Donate money to a charity in the memory of your loved one.
- Wear the jewelry or a trinket they used to wear as a remembrance.
- Start a scholarship in their name.
- Memorialize and celebrate your loved ones online. There are sites that offer a meaningful way to celebrate the life of a loved one with family and friends wherever they are. By creating some type of remembrance, you can add your thoughts in words, pictures, and video to other memorials. Because of the Internet, it is possible to be part of the ceremony of one's passing without physically being there.
- Look at old photos with a friend.
- Have a church service said in their memory.
- Bake or cook their favorite food and tell stories while you eat it.
- Light a virtual candle in their memory.
- Make a quilt using their clothes. My sister coordinated this and presented us with two quilts—one from Jenelle's clothes and one from Amy's. We proudly display these in our house. Try to change the death taboo by teaching others that it is OK to talk about death and dying.
- Make a memory box. Char made each girl a memory box that includes a picture of each girl, an article of clothing, a favorite book of each, and their graduation certificates. These memory boxes still hang in our house today and will for the rest of our lives.

Amy's Memory Box

Jenelle's Memory Box

Favorite book–Captain
Underpants

Quincy High School Diploma

Favorite SweatShirt

Girls Rule Hat

On my birthday, I like to
swim and have fun!

Blood Donor Card

Picture with a Pet Rabbit

First License Plate

Section 2

Helping others that are grieving
Am I helping or hurting?

Most of us jump right in when a friend or family member is hurting. Sometimes we do not plan what to do or say, we just do or say the first thing that comes to our mind. This thought process is not always in the best interest of the griever.

A different approach is to ask yourself—

"What does this loss mean to this person at this time?"

Or

"How does what I do or say affect my friend, the griever?"

If you start by asking yourself one of these questions, you will be in a much better position to help, not hurt your friend.

Oftentimes, we are in a position where we need to provide some sort of comfort and support to a friend or family member who is grieving. What we have learned is that there is a right way and a wrong way to provide this type of help.

First, let us start with the terminology. Please do not ever assume that you are "dealing" with or "handling" a griever. These cliché terms or buzzwords are quite overused and worthless. Other words like closure and healing are also overused. Our good friend, Becky, compared the use of dealing with grieving people" like dealing with a skunk under your front porch or a hornet's nest in your backyard. Grievers are real people with unbelievable burdens and pain to bear. Becky encourages us to use the words "helping or consoling" or to provide "solace" to the griever instead of using the words "dealing with".

With that in mind, grievers do not need to **be dealt with**, they need to be handled gently and compassionately, consoled, and listened to. Keep this as lesson number one. We need to eliminate the term "dealing with" when it comes to helping those that are grieving.

Grievers can feel cast out or banished from their own communities. It is not fair, and it is not true in most cases. However, sometimes family and friends tend to "drift away" or push away from those who are grieving. You are probably telling yourself right now "this would never happen to me. I would never abandon my friend." I hope that you are right. However, sometimes, even good friends become uncomfortable around our grief.

Some of my best friends in the world simply quit supporting me several months after the accident. Did it hurt? Absolutely. Are they still great friends? Yes, they are.

My unrealistic expectations were that good friends and family would reach out to me with good thoughts or stories about the girls–**<u>forever</u>**. I still feel angry that some family members do not call or send us something on July 22 each year. I know that they have not forgotten Jenelle, Amy, or Mom. What I am trying to say is that sometimes grievers, like me, have unrealistic expectations from others.

Jenelle and Amy were extremely involved with both church and school activities. As parents, we spent most of the time with the parents of the girls' friends. After they died, we noticed that many of these people chose not to be around Char and me as much as they once were. Why? Because they were uncomfortable with our grief. Our normal conversations would involve what our children were doing. That conversation stopped immediately for us on July 22, 2003.

Many of our friends and family were concerned about upsetting us and watching us "break into tears". We did that frequently. They were also concerned about themselves—as much as we were. In our culture, most people confront uncomfortable situations awkwardly and even hurtfully. They choose not to embarrass themselves by either doing or saying the wrong thing. Thus, they choose to say or do nothing.

Ignoring a griever can cause as much or more pain than not knowing what to say when you do see them. Some people thought they were sneaky and pretended not to see us. Perhaps they would turn around and head to the other side of the store. Most people are not like James Bond—meaning they are not very sneaky.

Char remembers a time at a grocery store seeing a mother and daughter from Amy's soccer team. She looked forward to visiting with them. Then, they simply pretended that they did not see her, so they did not have to speak with her. This really hurt my wife. I am sure those people meant well but were uncomfortable being around a grieving mother and did not realize how much they hurt Char. This type of event happened many times to both Char and me over the first few years. We decided to write this book to help people better understand how to help or comfort grievers. Hugs really do help.

There are also stories of total strangers reaching out to us. We received mail from all over the country from people saying that they were both thinking about us and praying for us. We also had numerous people ask, "Can I give you a hug? They had heard of our loss and simply wanted to help share the pain for a few seconds.

I remember a time in 2004 when I was on a business trip to Texas. I was in an office preparing for a meeting with the owner of the company when a total stranger asked me if she could give me a BIG HUG. I did not know this person at all, but gladly received her hug. She told me that she had heard about our loss from somebody at work and that she was praying for my family and me. She knew that we were grieving, sensed my pain, and wanted to help. Although I specifically remember this instance, it happened frequently to Char and me.

You have heard the saying "reach out and touch someone." When you know of someone who is struggling with their grief, I encourage you to do just that because, HUGS HELP.

My mother, Jean, became a golfer after she retired. This surprised all her children because she had never been golfing before. Mom always tried to make things fun. She always brought a bag of candy to the golf course. At the fifth tee box, she would open the candy and share it with her fellow golfers. After mom passed, the golf course purchased a bench in Mom's honor, placed it on the fifth tee, and called it "Candy Time", in honor of Mom.

We heard stories like these for years. If you want to help make this a better world, try reaching out to somebody that you do not know and show him or her that you do care. It will make a big difference for that person.

The next time that you are in a situation like this, do something very simple like—give them a hug or shake their hand. All you have to say is "I've been thinking about you and praying for you and your family".

I encourage you to try this—reach out and touch someone that you do not know. Send them a card, bring them something, or simply give them a hug and say that you are thinking about them. It meant the world to us, and it will mean the world to others as well.

Most of us learned how to acquire or gather things, not what to do when we lose them. In our early years, we try to acquire friendship, love, and acceptance. As we get older, we learn how to acquire assets or expensive toys like boats and campers. Advertising and marketing campaigns are all about getting personal belongings into our hands. Sometimes, friends and close family members take the same approach. Now, what happens when somebody close to you dies? Most of us do not know how to react or what to say or do. You can learn how to cook or mow or dance or drive—there are tools and training to help with all of these. Have you ever seen any training courses on "How to grieve?" or "How to help others with their grief?" Probably not. Some of us learned to ignore grief. Char's family took the approach. If you do not talk about it, maybe you will forget about it.

Chapter 14

The Thoughtful Caregiver
Provide Provide options, not advice

Sometimes when we try to help our grieving friends or family members, we say or do the wrong things. Most of us try to "fix the problem" by offering solutions or advice.

Below are several examples of unwanted advice we received from friends, family, and co-workers that wanted to help but did not know how to. Some of the BAD ADVICE we heard included:

- Do not spend so much time by yourself.
- Try to be alone when you are grieving. Which one is it?
- What is done is done. (No idea what this meant)
- Be sure to do your "grief work" (whatever that is)
- Time heals all wounds—Means just give it time
- You must move on
- Never burden others with your feelings
- Eat better and exercise more (Sounds like a real doctor)
- Be sure to take your medicine
- Be strong for others
- Join a club or volunteer at the hospital. Maybe this will allow you to focus less on your pain.
- Quit crying or quit grieving—it has been almost two weeks (This was one of my favorites).

It is important to understand that what you have learned about grieving in the past is probably not correct. Instead of relying on old ideas and urban myths, try to think about what is happening right in front of you. If you lost a loved one, and somebody told you to "Move on", what would you do?

Offering advice and solutions to a grieving person is simply a way to try to "fix the problem". I believe that most people say these things because they have heard them from others. Unless you have suffered a similar loss, you cannot possibly have any idea of what they are going through. These sayings and expressions come off as uncaring and even insulting. The griever probably feels like you are trying to minimize their pain. It is like saying "Quit feeling sorry for yourself".

Empathy is "trying to put yourself in someone else's shoes. In my case, unless someone has lost a young child, how can they understand what I am going through?

What we learned that helped us was when people provided us options, not advice. Nobody likes being told what to do—especially somebody who is grieving. When you are in this situation—and want to help your friend—make some suggestions or options. Examples include:

- Have you thought about seeing a counselor? I have heard that both Bettie Sue and Bobbie Lou are great grief counselors. Would you like me to get you their contact information?
- I know that you are very much against taking any type of depression medicine. So am I. However, I encourage you to keep an open mind about it. Please consider talking to your doctor about it.
- I cannot imagine the stress you are under at work. Have you considered asking your manager for some additional time off?
- I have read that some people prefer to talk about their loss vs. keeping the pain inside of them. Would you like to talk about Jenelle and Amy?

You get the idea—Offer options, not advice.

Chapter 15

The Thoughtful Caregiver
Talk about the deceased person

Urban myth: Never mention the loss of a loved
one. **WRONG. WRONG. WRONG.**

Always Remember—we want our loved ones remembered forever. I
encourage you to ask the griever if you can share a story about their loved
one. If they say they are not yet ready, honor their wishes.

Why do we not mention the loss? Mostly, because we are all scared of
making a mistake and upsetting our friends. Unbelievably, by doing this,
you are most likely upsetting your friend that is grieving even more.

First, the griever is already in a confused state of mind. They have not
forgotten that their friend or family member recently died. They never
will. However, if you fail to mention the loss, it is like a slap in the face
to the griever. It leaves them alone with their feelings and tells them that
you have either forgotten about their loved one or that their grieving and
distress is not welcome in your presence.

A good friend of mine lost his son in a gun accident in 1987. Ten years later
a good friend stopped by and shared a picture of their son they found when
going through a family picture album. The friend also shared a funny story
of what they remember about him. Even ten years later, this sharing of a
picture and a story about his deceased son still meant a lot to my friend.

These types of memories are so important to those suffering from loss. It does not matter when you share these types of stories, as it is always a great memory.

Jenelle and Amy died on July 22, 2003. Char and I still love to hear stories about them. Sometimes we start the conversation and ask others to join in. Your friends will as well. It is an important part of the healing process.

Below are some personal stories that helped us to Survive and Remember

It is always better to share a story, bring a picture, or at least mention the deceased person than to ignore the loss.

Our friends gathered stories about Mom, Jenelle, and Amy and shared them with us. We put all these stories into a "memory book". I never realized how often we would reach for this picture and storybook. It helped me to realize that no matter how bleak things may look, we would never forget the amazing lives of these three. By putting these memories and stories on paper, we can go back and recall the fun times we had and to remind ourselves that their lives were short-lived, but amazing.

At the girl's funeral, we asked the attendees to share stories about Jenelle and Amy. Did we cry when we heard them, absolutely? Most people did. However, we still remember those stories to this day. Below are a couple of them.

About Amy

This is Amy's casket right after it was closed after the visitation. This was the last time I ever saw my daughter. I did not want to leave the funeral home that night.

My sister, Jill, wrote the following about Amy.

How do you describe a child who only had nine short years on this earth? She was a child who had a world of things to give, just not enough time. She was caring and compassionate, always wanting to help those in need. She was the organizer when all the kids got together. She figured out the best games to play, the most fun way to do something, how to put together a show for all the adults to watch (she would write the script, choreograph the other kids' movements-everything). She was so talented and very smart. I always thought that of all the nieces and nephews, Amy would be the one to become famous. She loved being the center of attention and was not shy when it came to performing for others.

Amy always surprised people with how articulate she was. She could carry on a lively adult conversation, while at the same time play with other kids. Writing was easy for her. She liked to please others, something that was not hard with her sunny disposition. Rarely was there not a beautiful smile on Amy's face.

Many people will now unknowingly miss out on something wonderful and positive in their lives-meeting and knowing Amy Stocker. She never got the chance to be the best friend, lover, wife, mother, and grandmother she would have become.

All four of Amy's grade schoolteachers, along with the school principal attended both the funeral and the visitation. One of them stood up and told the following story about Amy:

It was in the early winter and most of the teachers had the flu. We were very short on substitute teachers for the same reason. Amy was in third grade at the time. One of the teachers suggested to the principal that Amy Stocker teach her own third grade class. This spoke so highly of Amy. We loved hearing this story about how our daughter stood out in the minds of her teachers.

To further honor Amy, the school created an Amy Stocker Memorial Award and presented it annually to a deserving third grade student at Madison Elementary School who exhibited strong leadership, character, optimism, and service to others. This was our Amy—a true leader at age nine.

The Amy Stocker Memorial Award. Presented annually
to a deserving 3rd Grader at Madison
Elementary School who exhibits strong leadership,
character, optimism, & service to others.

The principal at her school asked Char and me to hand out this award to the winners each year up until 2017. The teachers would tell the third graders about this award at the beginning of each year and would use the criterion to help grow more leaders like Amy Stocker.

Another story came from Amy's second grade teacher, Molly Stroot. Her thoughts included:

"I have been teaching for 19 years and rarely have I had the privilege to be touched by someone like Amy Stocker. The moment I met her; I knew that she was an exceptional child. Amy excelled in all subjects in school and was sure to be a tremendous success in whatever she would do. She had the drive and the motivation to always do her best and always help others. Her caring attitude was evident each day…always asking to help those who seemed to struggle. Amy was intensely liked and admired by all her classmates.

Amy had what we all want in life. She had a positive outlook on everything she did. She saw the good in everything. She reached for the stars and never gave up. Her heart was so big and so full, but she continued to fill it with more and more friends and more and more love. Amy was a loving girl who wanted to give more than to receive.

Leadership. That is a strong word, and it fits Amy perfectly. She was a leader. Her morals and ethics were always evident in her daily life; always trying to do what was right. I called her the "other teacher" in which she grinned and nodded her head. Amy was extraordinary in her maturity, wanting to take others under her wing.

To think that this little girl, so full of life and love, and was taken from us at such a young age is devastating. Amy had so much to look forward to in her life. She would have been a tremendous asset to our community and to our world. She would have done well every day of her life. This good would only spill unto others, making others' lives fulfilling as well. Every time I think of Amy, I see a smile. I see a warm, true smile that generates true happiness with herself, her family, and her friends. This loss is immeasurable.

Amy is continuing to inspire me as a teacher. Each day, I dedicate my day to her... striving to become a more empathetic and caring teacher. She is my inspiration and will always be in my heart".

Thank you, Mrs. Stroot.

Stories like these kept us going. Nevertheless, it is not just about us. Every loss has stories that the griever wants and needs to hear. Help your friends by putting stories in writing that they can read and cherish for the rest of their lives—just like this one from Amy's teacher. If you choose not to put your stories in writing, be sure to remind them of their loved one whenever you can.

About Jenelle

Here is Jenelle's casket. Hundreds of people from all over came
to share their thoughts and stories about Jenelle and Amy.

The note below came from my sister, Jill Reid—the aunt of Jenelle and Amy.

How do you start writing a letter to describe how important two nieces were in your life? The value of their life, as far as I am concerned, is immeasurable. They were both such a tremendous joy to be around. They were happy—always. They were kind—always. They were good, polite, funny, and entertaining. How can I put a value on the time we had together? The word "Priceless" would be the only way to describe it. Too short, for sure.

The pain of their loss is such a deep pain-a hurt so deep in my soul; it cannot be explained to someone. It can only be felt in accompaniment with losing someone—three someone's in my case-that meant the world to me and to so many other people.

I was 17 when Jenelle was born-a senior in High School. She was the oldest of the grandchildren, so with her birth, I became an aunt for the first time. She was a beautiful baby and a gorgeous little girl. Even as a little child, Jenelle was caring and giving. She sang a lot and talked a lot and had a way of cheering up anyone who was around.

As Jenelle grew older, I became increasingly proud of her. I was so proud of how sure she was of herself. She knew who she was and what she wanted out of life, and she did everything in her power to achieve her goals. If she wanted to buy something, she would get a job and raise money for it. She was one of the few individuals I've ever met that was completely comfortable with who she was—and proud of who she was. Peer pressure didn't seem to be a problem for her. When others were doing things that she didn't agree with, she would simply say "No thanks, that's not for me".

Jenelle was a very talented artist. I was amazed by her drawings and how easily drawing came to her. She was studying to be an architect and my nine-year-old son was planning on following in her footsteps. After her death, he said to me, "Now I can't become an architect. I was going to learn all about how to become one from Jenelle and now she's gone, and I can't." From his young viewpoint, losing his role model meant losing his dreams as well.

<u>Thoughts about Mom</u>

Mom had her own burial site in Gibson City, IL. We created
this additional stone and kept it in Quincy. We knew that
mom and the girls were all together in heaven.

Somebody set up a website after Mom, Jenelle, and Amy died. Some of the feedback from that website included:

"Anybody else feel like there is now a great big void in Gibson City? What a waste, and truly a damn shame. Jean was one of those folks that when you saw her come in a room, the whole mood brightened. She was one of a kind. She had a heart of gold. She will be sorely missed".

"Jean was like having another grandmother to look after me. I miss her smile and her sense of humor. She was such a great person. It's so hard to believe she is gone."

Picture of Mom and Dad along with fourteen grandchildren. Mom was an amazing
mother and grandmother. Jenelle is the tall one by Grandpa. Amy is the one standing
in the middle. These grandchildren had so much fun together.

My point in sharing these stories about Jenelle, Amy, and Mom with you is to let you know how important it is to do something extra for a friend in grieving. It is something they will remember for the rest of their lives. We certainly do.

If you want to do something special for your grieving friend, try to come up with something with heartfelt meaning and sincerity. They will treasure it for years to come. Please go the extra mile for your friend or family member and do something that shows that you will <u>always remember</u>.

Grandma Jean with her first grandchild, Jenelle

Chapter 16

Never Forget
More than words are needed
Really. Hugs do cure tears

As I shared earlier, avoiding discussing the loss of a child or other loved one is a mistake. It is important to use pictures and events to help remember the deceased. I remember that Char's parents chose to hide all the pictures of Jenelle and Amy at their house. They thought it was important not to "dwell" on the past and always look forward. Char said that growing up they did not talk about things like "death". When they removed the pictures of the girls, they thought that they were helping us, not hurting us. I strongly encouraged them to put the pictures back in the main room. At the time, I did not understand their thought process at all. Pretending that Jenelle and Amy were not part of our past by not displaying their pictures was ridiculous. Although Char understood why they were doing it, it really "made me angry".

Mack and Delores, Char's parents, were amazing people. I just did not realize that culturally, there were many differences in how people grieve and talk about death. This might be something to consider when comforting friends that are grieving. Ask yourself questions like, "how were they raised?" and "how was death viewed?" Mack and Delores never talked much about Jenelle and Amy after they passed. They were always calm and not excitable about much of anything. I believe Char called them "stoic".

Char and I grieved so differently mainly because we came from different family cultures. My family always talked about everything. I was always a very emotional person.

Char's family was clearly uncomfortable crying and expressing their feelings. It was very difficult for me to understand, but, to this day, I respect their family culture. Even when her mom passed, "don't cry" and "be strong" were the messages she heard. Even though she lost her daughters, she would have to be strong. Mack and Delores raised her this way.

We continued to attend the same events that we attended with Jenelle and Amy. We always hoped that others would either mention the girls or tell a story about them or at least state they miss them. We were usually disappointed as most people took the "ignore them" approach.

I know that I have mentioned this a few times, but it is vitally important that you share some type of story in writing about your friend's loss. We read these stores at least twice per year—and usually cry when reading them. However, it really means a lot to us and helps us to remember how wonderful Mom, Jenelle, and Amy were and how much they meant to friends and family.

To keep their memories alive, several things happened including:

- Donating money on behalf of the girls—it was always important to them to help others. They knew they had a great home and a loving family. They also knew that many others were not as fortunate as they were. Based on this, we donated to the YWCA (Young Women's Christian Association) on behalf of Jenelle and Amy. The YWCA used the money to support their housing program that provided for local families to have a stable nurturing life while breaking the cycle of homelessness.

- Purchasing commemorative bricks at the Center for Women in Transition in support of the organization's building campaign. This organization provided housing and assistance to women and children that were experiencing homelessness in Champaign County. Our good friends Dave and Patti did this in memory of Mom, Jenelle, and Amy.

- Creating a Drury University Scholarship—The Jenelle M. Stocker Memorial Scholarship was established for four years and was given to a student that was in the Drury Architecture program, the same one that Jenelle was part of. Drury University also planted a tree and created a plaque in Jenelle's memory. Every time we are in the Springfield, MO area, we stop by to visit this unique memorial.

- The pageant directors at the Miss Quincy Scholarship Program created an award called, "The Essence Award". Each year an award went to one Miss Quincy and one Little Miss Quincy candidate that lived their platform while serving her community. Essence means both spirit and or character—of which both Jenelle and Amy both possessed. Both Jenelle and Amy participated in the Miss Quincy pageant in 2002. It was amazing to see both of our daughters in this pageant at the same time. The title of the pageant was "Angels Among Us". After they passed, the pageant leaders set up an "Angels among Us" annual scholarship program.

- Mom and Jenelle were both registered organ donors with the Red Cross and Illinois Eye Bank Transplant Centers at their deaths. Jenelle donated her corneas to a young man in Uniontown, Ohio. A sixteen-year-old boy in California who had four skin grafts in a spinal surgery and a 45-year-old man in Missouri were both recipients from her tissue donation. Because of our daughter, someone can see and two people had successful surgeries because of her tissue donation. Jenelle was still helping people after her death. Talk about a proud Papa.

- One of our friends gave us a tree in memory of Jenelle and Amy. At the time, we thought it was an unusual gift. However, we planted it with care and watched it begin to grow. When we moved, we made sure that this tree moved with us. When we decided to leave the state, we received permission to plant this tree at the cemetery—close to where Jenelle and Amy were buried. Every time we visit the girls at the cemetery, we check out that tree and are reminded of the nine and nineteen years that we were able to watch our daughters grow.

Chapter 17

The Thoughtful Caregiver

Be Smart in what you say

Have you ever noticed that most of us repeat things that we have heard in the past? Things like:

- They are in a better place
- How are you doing?
- God does not give you more that you can handle
- You will see them again in heaven.
- What does not kill you makes you stronger.
- At least they did not suffer
- I know how you feel
- Everything happens for a reason
- It was meant to be
- You are so strong, I could never handle this

These are all cliché's that most of us have heard before. Just because somebody else said them, we think they are OK to say. **WRONG!!!**

Thinking about what to say or what not to say may cause you to say nothing at all. The resulting silence can be very painful to the person who is grieving. Even though it may feel uncomfortable to say something, acknowledging your friend's loss is helpful and important to their healing process. The support of family and friends is a key consideration in how long and painful the grieving process may be. It also affects how somebody heals over time.

Below are some of the questions we received shortly after our loss. After each question, I tried to summarize my exact thoughts after hearing each question.

- **Never say "How are you doing?"** I heard people say these words many times after the accident. What did they think I was going to say? What I wanted to say was "what a stupid question! My two daughters and mom were just killed in an accident. I will never be able to see, hug, or talk with them–EVER AGAIN. How the hell do you think I am doing?" Dumb question!
- **Never say "They are in a better place"** We thought that our daughters were already in a great place, living with us. We have no doubt that heaven is wonderful and is a better place than our screwed-up world. However, we had a good thing going here on earth with Jenelle and Amy. Sure, we wanted them to go to heaven someday, but long after Char and I were there.

My brother told me about an episode in the television sitcom, Young Sheldon, when a teenager is killed driving a car. Young Sheldon's church-going mom cannot bring herself to tell the child's parents that their daughter is in a better place. She struggles to reconcile that sleeping in her own bed is where the child really needs to be-not in heaven. Char and I felt the same way—both then and now.

- **Never say "God does not give you more that you can handle"**
Our thoughts were that God really tested us by taking Jenelle, Amy, and Mom all at once. For a long time, I totally disagreed with this saying. Fortunately, we have been able to handle our loss and turned it around to help others that are grieving. Yes, God did not give us more than we could handle. It just took us several years to get to the point where we could handle our tremendous loss.

I will also note that I have family members who are still angry with God and the church that is supposed to represent Him on earth.

- **Never say "You will see them again in heaven".**

Our thoughts were and are that we cannot wait to see them again in heaven. Char and I read a couple of books that helped us understand how wonderful heaven is. "The Next Place" by Warren Hanson, is an inspirational journey of light and hope to a place where earthly hurts are left behind. Mr. Hanson talks about "an uncomplicated journey of awe and wonder to a destination without barriers." How can you not realize how wonderful heaven can be after reading words like these?

The other book we read multiple times was "A Travel Guide to Heaven" by Anthony DeStefano. This book describes heaven as spectacular sunsets, magnificent cities, fabulous beaches, exotic animals, and incredibly exciting people! According to Robin Leach, Lifestyles of the Rich and Famous, "they are all here in this marvelous new travel guide".

- **Never say "What does not kill you makes you stronger"**

We never quite figured out how this one applies to a grieving person. Whomever first said this statement apparently was not using it to describe somebody suffering from devastating grief after losing three family members. Our grief took away our strength for many years. We considered it progress when we were able to get out of bed in the morning and go to work each day. The loss destroyed our positive outlook on life. It did not physically kill us, but it did not make us stronger either. Even eighteen years later, we do not feel nearly as strong as we did before our loss.

- **Never say "At least they didn't suffer"**

How do you know they did not suffer? According to the first person at the accident scene, Amy was still alive for a few minutes after the accident. Can you honestly say that she "didn't suffer? How would anybody know? What a stupid thing to say! How about the potential for suffering a fraction of a second before the impact? What about the child killed by gunfire? Are they without even momentary suffering or unbridled fear? These are emotions you and I cannot possibly feel or understand given their situation.

- **Never say "Quit feeling sorry for yourself"**
I am not sure I would even want to have a friend that was so insensitive that he or she would say something like this. All that these sayings accomplish is to either deprive or invalidate the immense pain the griever is feeling.

We felt that these kinds of repeatable sayings were both hurtful and insulting at times. When trying to help or console a grieving person, try to speak to the current experience of your friend's overwhelming grief.

- **Never say "I know how you feel or I know what you are going through"**
How do you know how we feel? Have you experienced losing three family members at one time? Have you ever had to plan two funerals and two visitations within one week? Have you ever had to realize that you would never be able to hug your daughters again, **EVER**? You don't have a freakin' idea how we feel, and it really hurts us to even hear you say it.

Sayings like these devalue the griever's feelings. Mourners do not want to hear about others' experiences with grief. They need and want to be able to express their own. I had somebody that compared losing my daughters to his dog dying. Never-ever-ever say something like that. When he said it, it hurt terribly? It still hurts today.

- **Never say, "Everything happens for a reason."** I would challenge anybody in the world to come up with a "reason" why my nineteen and nine-year old daughters had to die like this.
- **Never say "It was meant to be"** "What was meant to be?" Why were my daughters involved in "meant to be?"

99

- **Never say "You are so strong, I could never handle this".** I am not sure that I can handle it either. However, I am the one that just suffered this terrible tragedy, and you are worried about yourself. WOW!!! I need your support and comfort, not your pity party.
- **Never compare your loss to your friend's loss.** Every loss is different and affects everybody differently. It is like comparing football to baseball. Both are great sports, but they are also unbelievably different.

What should I say?

How about?

- I cannot even imagine what you are going through.
- I do not know what to say, but I am here to help.
- I am so sorry for your loss. We are thinking about and praying for you and your family.
- I do not know what to say. I just want you to know that I am here for you.
- I am here for you and your family. I am here to listen to you if you need or want to talk.
- I am sorry that I cannot make things better for you.
- I cannot imagine that any expression of sympathy could be adequate or comforting. My thoughts and prayers are with you and your family members.
- No one can experience this sadness as you do, for your feelings are unique and very personal to you. No one can begin to know exactly how you feel, except to know that sorrow such as yours is deep, sad, and real. If you need some comfort and help to see you through, just know how loved and cared for you are by all those who think of you.
- You have lost someone very special to you. It is going to take time to ease the sadness you are feeling right now. May the fond recollections of all that you share together make tomorrow a little better and a little brighter.

Most of the time, you do not need to say anything. Just being there for your friend means so much to them. Remember, Hugs Help.

Sometimes it might help to share a brief memory by personalizing your thoughts. For example:

- I heard about your **mom**. I am so sorry for your loss. I will always remember her beautiful smile.
- So sorry to hear about your **father**. I will never forget all the fun we had when he took us on that fishing trip.
- I am so sorry for your loss. **Amy** was a great soccer player. All of us miss her.
- **Frank**, I am so sorry about your wife. She was an amazing actress and director. I am still amazed by what she did with "Joseph and the Amazing Technicolor Dreamcoat".

Statements like these show your focus on your friend and that you are open to talking to them about their grief. Simply ask them what they are feeling and then listen to what they say. Never try to fix it. It is also OK to say nothing. The process of being there as they grieve, whether it be providing a hug, holding their hand, or simply sitting with them can help with the healing process. One of my brothers has often shared that there are no words to provide relief to the griever.

It is much more important for you to listen and try to understand what the griever is going through at that minute in time. Our society places so much value on the ability to "carry on" or "keep your chin up " or "keep busy" or "It's time to get on with your life." These messages encourage grievers to deny or repress their grief rather than to express it. Please try to avoid these "cliché messages" as they tend to hurt more than they help.

Grief is an inevitable part of life. At some point in everybody's lifetime, there is going to be some grieving involved. If you see a friend or family member grieving, it can often be hard to grasp how to best support them.

Ask yourself these questions:

- What type of support does my friend need? Do they need emotional support? Do they need physical support? Do they need financial support? Do they just need somebody to listen?

- How can I be supportive without overstepping the boundaries? This is an area to choose caution. You do not want to be telling your friend what to do or when to do it. That is overstepping. Be very careful in this area.
- If I were in this situation, how would I feel or what would mean the most to me?

Ask the griever these questions:

- What can you tell me about your loved one? It could be very helpful for them to reminisce or share some stories.
- What type of support have you been getting from your family and friends? Sometimes the support from family and friends has not been as strong as expected or needed. This question sometimes leads to a better discussion of what the griever needs.
- If you need to broach a specific subject like the funeral service or about a money situation, try to use an open ended approach like 'How are you feeling about the planning for the funeral service?' or "How are you feeling about your money situation?"
- What are you worried about and what can I do to help?

Chapter 18

Tips on how to support a grieving friend

When a friend or family member loses a loved one, helping them through their time of grief is one of the most supportive and loving things a person can do. Ideas include:

- **BE AN ACTIVE LISTENER AND LISTEN WITHOUT JUDGMENT**

One of the most important things you can do for a grieving friend is to listen to them without interruption. When you listen, never judge their feelings, or try to console them. Instead, just let them talk through their grief with as few distractions as possible. Do not be tempted to offer advice. Grieving is not something that needs to be fixed or that can be fixed. It is something that changes in a regular and repeated way. Your friend must know that you are there to support them for as long as it takes. It is important to recognize their ideas and concerns and encourage them to talk about their feelings. Empathize with their problems and let them know you are always there to listen to what they are going through.

- **HELP THEM FIND MEANING AGAIN**

It can be hard for somebody to find meaning again after a loss. It is and can be a very personal thing. As a friend, be sure to understand that the grieving process is unique for everyone. Some people find meaning through their church and religion, while others find themselves questioning their once deeply held beliefs. Some approaches to take to help someone find meaning include:

- **HELP THEM TO REALIZE THE SHORTNESS OF LIVE AS WELL AS THE VALUE OF LIFE.**

Unfortunately, life does not always last as long as we want it to. Try to get them thinking about the amazing times they had with their loved one before they passed. I thank God every day for the nineteen and nine years I had with Jenelle and Amy.

- **HELP THEM TO REALIZE THE LOVE AND SUPPORT THEY ARE RECEIVING FROM FRIENDS AND FAMILY.**

Sometimes they are so buried in their own grief; they forget to appreciate the efforts and hard work of others who are supporting them.

- **HELP THEM TO CREATE SOMETHING TO MEMORIALIZE THE LIFE OF THE DECEASED.**

This could be something as simple as a shadow box with a picture of their loved one in it or a piece of clothing. We added a copy of their favorite books in our shadow boxes.

- **HELP THEM TO HONOR THEIR LOVED ONES**

Help them to honor their loved ones by treating others as they did or helping others who are grieving.

Some find it helpful to seek out a grief support group where they can talk with other people who are experiencing similar things. Others find meaning in gardening, bicycling, travel, or prayer.

The grieving process never really ends – it is something people learn to live with every day. Be there to support your friend as they try to find meaning in life even amid their grief.

- **BE THERE WHEN THEY NEED YOU – BUT KNOW YOUR LIMITS TOO**

At first, the griever will most likely need lots of support from their family and friends. It is so important for you to be visible and available during these times. After a while, it is OK to decrease your time spent with them and allow them to grieve on their own. Simply make sure they know that you are available to them at any time.

Keep in mind the tremendous amount of attention the griever will get shortly after the death and burial of their loved one. It can go from non-stop people bringing food and visiting with them to utter silence. This happened to us. Suddenly, it was just Char, Matt, and me in this big house. Where were all the people? Where did all our friends go? It was just a major change in a short time.

My advice is to be more proactive a couple of weeks after the funeral. Let your friend know that you still care and are still available to talk and visit. Your friend will really need you at first and they will really need your love and support after a few weeks when all the activity dies down.

Many bereaved people claim that months and even years after the loss, people stop showing up or showing that they care. This is often out of fear of bringing up the past and causing pain for a grieving person. Everything is a balancing act. Bringing up the past might cause some pain but forgetting to bring it up will cause pain for sure. There is nothing wrong with asking whether it hurts or helps when you bring up the name of the deceased.

We appreciated the many notes and cards that we received months after the accident. We continue to receive "thinking of you" cards and emails on the anniversary of the girl's death.

- **DO NOT OVERDO IT!**

It is important to give your friend some space to allow them to deal with the grief on their own. Just because they need you, it does not mean they want you there all the time. Sometimes, what they really need is a chance to deal with their grief on their own terms.

On the other hand, if you are positive that your friend will always welcome your support and presence, do not ignore it! It means a lot when someone stands with us in trying times.

- **OFFER TO HELP WITH EVERYDAY TASKS AND ERRANDS**

Simple acts of friendship mean so much to somebody who is grieving. Just because it appears that they are doing OK with their grief on the outside, it does not mean that internally they are doing well at all.

Char and I went back to work a couple of weeks after the girls died. Yes, we were able to do our jobs and it appeared that we were doing OK. **That was not the case.** People thought that something was wrong with Char because she was back at work, not crying nonstop, and appearing to function OK. Despite doing my job, I was breaking down multiple times each day, struggling to concentrate, and hating life. Besides that, we really did not like each other very much because we were grieving so differently, and our world was falling apart.

The perception that someone is doing OK can be the wrong observation. It is easy for someone to appear OK. Despite the outward appearances, people had no idea that we were crying frequently, rarely eating or sleeping, and frustrated and angry most of the time.

A friend told Char that she did not need to "put on a brave face" for them. That was a very kind thing for them to share with her because, of course, she was hurting deeply and trying to "be brave".

You can help your friend by asking if they need any help in completing any small tasks around the home or office. They might decline at first, but later realize that you are helping and appreciate your presence. Sometimes, it is the company they are looking for, and not the help. We always were so happy when somebody would drop by the house and bring us a meal or ask if we wanted to go on a walk. There are numerous ways to help people in need. Just because they say they do not need your help the first time, does not mean they will not appreciate your help in the future.

Overall, it is essential not to rush things along or force people into talking about their grief before they are ready. Make sure that you are giving them space to process this difficult time on their own and provide gentle reminders occasionally that you are always there for them if they need it.

Chapter 19

Helping Children to Grieve

Many young people attended both the funeral and visitation for Jenelle and Amy. As these children-mostly under the age of twenty, came through the lines, I felt so sorry for them and their parents. Yes, we were struggling with our own loss, but the death of Jenelle and Amy affected numerous other classmates, friends, and fellow athletes. How does a parent explain the death of a nine-year-old to her best friends? How did the death of nineteen-year-old Jenelle affect her college classmates? Kids this age pretty much think they are indestructible. Attending the visitation and funeral of a fellow student had to be difficult for them.

We admitted not fully understanding what was going on in Matt's mind. He was seventeen at the time. He remembers the following:

- Worrying about Char and me because we were not eating at all.
- Worrying about money and being concerned that we might lose our house.
- Sharing his thoughts and emotions to a group of teenagers at a TEC (Teens Encounter Christ) conference.
- Crying so hard when driving that he had to pull the car over.
- Spending more time with friends than with family.
- Chasing girls—this was a good distraction for him.
- Sleeping with a special blanket that Grandma Jean had made for him. When a friend said that it looked "store bought", Matt got mad and threw him out of the house.

- Learning to play the guitar in honor of Jenelle who had recently started playing. (The first song that he played was at Amy's birthday party when he played "Happy Birthday" for his baby sister.
- Hearing Jenelle's boyfriend, Dave, making a loud and scary noise when he saw her body at the visitation. Matt thought he had just heard "the sound of true pain". It was inhuman sounding and really scared him.
- Not blaming God for their death. When a good friend died with a brain aneurysm, he was upset and did blame God. He strictly blamed the truck driver for the deaths of his sisters.

We had no idea Matt was concerned about things like money and our health. If you are in this situation, please reach out better than we did to understand what is going through the mind of your children. We talk about "everybody grieves differently". This applies to children of all ages as well.

Schools and crisis response workers in many parts of the country have helped children cope with the concept of death because of the war or acts of terror. Some children are suffering a personal loss. Others will have a heightened fear of death because either they are worried about further attacks, or they have family members in the military, active reserves, or public safety roles. Some children may simply be more aware of death and try to sort through their feelings and thoughts.

Death is a reality of life faced by everyone, even children. As much as parents and other adults might want to protect children from death, we simply cannot. Please do not assume that because children are not talking about death, they are not thinking about it either. Whether we discuss it with them or not, children are aware of death. Since they are aware of it, we need to help them understand and cope with this reality.

When a friend dies, children must accomplish multiple tasks with the help of an adult to assure that their grief will be "good grief". Some of these tasks include:

1. Understanding–make sure they understand that the deceased is no longer alive and will never be a part of the child's life in the physical sense.
2. Grieving–help them work through the various feelings that are part of mourning. Make sure they understand that everybody grieves differently and that it is OK.
3. Remembering–the life and friendship by doing things such as planting a tree in memory of the deceased or celebrating their "birthdays in heaven" each year.

Some thoughts to consider when sharing the news of the death of a friend or family member with a young child.

1. Expect many questions, not only about the death, but also about the overall life cycle. Be prepared with your own thoughts about a particular death before trying to answer a child's questions.
2. Keep the lines of communication as open as possible. At first, provide only the basic information such as who died and what happened.
3. Answer truthfully. Try to speak at the child's level of understanding. Make sure to provide both consistent and complete information. Tell the truth.
4. Clarify the questions by repeating them only providing the basic information to answer those questions. Nothing more.
5. Try not to confuse the child by using words like "sleeping, passed on, or gone on a trip". Be specific by using easily understood words like dead and stopped breathing. Some of these other words describe something that is reversible to a young person. For example, going to heaven is not very different from going to Chicago.
6. Encourage the child to express their feelings about what happened. If possible, try to address a child's unspoken feelings as well. Sadness is the most obvious emotion to expect after a loss, but not the only one. Some may cry, some may continue playing, some may retreat into silence, and some may simply not believe you. It is also important to explain why others are expressing their feelings about the loss.

Chapter 20

The Thoughtful Caregiver

BE PROACTIVE

Most of us are trying to be helpful in these situations. We want to be there for our friends and family, but do not know what to do or say. We got so tired of hearing people say, "If you need anything, just call" or "please call me if I can help".

Unfortunately, most offers of help were vague and non-specific. Grievers need absolutes, not generalized promises. We heard things like:

- If you need your yard mowed, let me know. A better thing to do—If you really want to help, drive by my house. If my grass needs cutting, cut it. I am not going to ask you to mow my yard simply because I am grieving. I did not ask you to do this before my loss, and I am not going to ask you now.
- If you feel like going out to lunch, call me. When grieving, you usually feel like talking to someone. You should not have to "reach out or call" a good friend. They already know that you need to eat at least three meals a day. A good friend should simply show up and take you to lunch.

Specific offers of help are much less stressful to the grieving person. Instead of having to think of a response to your generic offer, like "What can I do to help?" simply provide a choice.

People that have suffered unimaginable loss need absolutes in their life. I remember one time that a good friend promised to stop by my house at 5:00 p.m. to visit and maybe drown our sorrows together. I was excited about this promise and really looked forward to our get together. I needed to talk to somebody. When he did not show, it was like another major setback. Grievers have already suffered a major disappointment in their lives. Whenever possible, help them to avoid anymore times of disillusionment or discouragement. If you make a promise to a griever, be as specific as you can and **MAKE IT HAPPEN!** Otherwise, your friend will be forlorn once again.

Chapter 21

The Thoughtful Caregiver
Think of the griever, not of yourself

Sometimes, we forget who is grieving. Instead of trying to help the griever, we are simply trying to help ourselves through our own grief. We heard things like:

- This has shattered my world
- I have not been able to sleep since I heard your news
- I have been crying non-stop

If you really want to help your friend, concentrate on his or her emotions or situation, not yours. I truly believe that it is extremely important that you get your personal feelings out and talk to somebody that can help you. However, do not expect that help to come from the person that you are supposed to be helping. Sharing your feelings with the griever is asking them to take care of you, while during their own pain and suffering. Your need for comfort does not help.

I remember on numerous occasions where friends and family who were trying to help broke out into tears and anger. We appreciated their passion and frustration, but it was hard enough to take care of our own personal needs without having to console them at the same time.

We had separate visitations for Mom and the girls. It seemed like thousands of people attended each visitation. We truly appreciated everybody that stopped by, but by the end of each event, I felt that I was consoling the people that came to console my family and me. NOT RIGHT! I left each event thinking, "who just lost three members of their family?"

My advice is that if you are not strong enough to control your own emotions in front of your grieving friends, stay away until you are strong enough.

- **This has shattered my world.** My thoughts were "are you kidding"? I am so sorry that my loss has shattered your world. How about you "get a life" and think about what we are going through? I would never say or think this now, but back when I was grieving, I sure thought it.
- **I have not been able to sleep since I heard your news.** My thoughts were that I am sorry that you are not sleeping well. However, if you were truly a friend, you would be more concerned about how my family and me are feeling and sleeping.
- **I have been crying non-stop.** My thoughts are "me too." I am in so much pain right now that I do not have the energy or time to worry about you.

Chapter 22

How to be a true friend to a griever

"A real friend is one who walks in when the rest of the world walks out. Don't walk in front of me, I may not follow. Don't walk behind me, I may not lead. Walk beside me and be my friend". –Charles Caleb Colton

What a great saying! It gets right to the heart of what grievers really need—a good, true friend that provides needed empathy in an unconditional way. Grief has a way of sorting out those who remain "true friends" vs. those who just disappear.

Ask yourself–did your relationship with your friend change because their profound grief was not comfortable for you or was it something more? If you have not figured it out yet, not everybody who was a good friend before will continue to be a good friend after your loss.

Ask yourself "who changed, my friend or me?"

Unfortunately, as part of our grieving process, our personal wants and needs as well as our priorities change. Sometimes our old friends have no interest or are not capable of meeting our new wants and needs.

Being a friend to a grieving person is something that you need to understand, practice, and perfect. WE ARE DIFFERENT! It is helpful to understand that grievers may need some of all of the following:

- They need to hear the name of their loved one. (Examples of what to say). "Randy, I was thinking about the time that Jenelle and Amy were in the Miss Quincy beauty pageant. They were so beautiful up on that stage". What a great memory to bring up. Another relative said, "I really was impressed the way Amy played the game of basketball at such a young age. I'll bet she could have been a champion in high school, and maybe even college".

- They need to be able to tell their story and share how they are hurting. (Example of what to say), "I want to be able to help you. Please tell me how you are feeling and what I could make you feel better"?

- They need to talk about their grieving experiences to a great listener, not to a great fixer. (Example of what to say) Oftentimes people talk more than they listen. "Right now, I want to be able to hear what you have to say, and I promise to be a GREAT Listener".

To be a better friend, ask yourself these questions:

- Am I someone that my friend can confide in and trust with his/her most personal thoughts and feelings?

- Am I someone who is not judgmental and allows them to say what they need to say when they need to say it?

- Am I someone who is there when others walk away?

- Am I someone who is a great listener that can accept their quiet times and tears, without judgment?

- Am I someone who will remain in contact with you and will spend as much time as you need, for as long as you need it?

Section 3

God, Church, and Grieving

Chapter 23

Religion and spirituality

Grief and loss may also cause a person to question his or her faith or view of the world. Alternatively, it may strengthen the person's faith by providing a new understanding of the meaning of life. Char and I saw both sides.

Church and Our Story

This is a hard subject to discuss. Mostly, because Char and I grieved so differently and because neither one of us was very happy with the support we received from our church.

For Char, the church is her anchor. It was always her family's anchor and her grandparents' anchor. It is a big social activity for her family. They were always very involved in the church. It has been and will always be a big part of her life.

After the girls died, we went to church that first Sunday and someone asked us, "what are you doing here"? Char's response was "It is Sunday. I mean, why would I miss church?" This friend thought that we should be home crying. Since she grew up Catholic, you always go to church; you do not skip to church. When she felt lonely and lost and was very depressed, she knew and trusted that God had her back. "You know, people can die, but I've always got Jesus" was something Char told me.

When something tragic happens, we all react differently. Our religion plays a big part in how we deal with death and grieving. My beautiful wife spent many hours at church after the accident. She wanted and needed to be near God. It was very important to her.

Not me.

I tried very hard to go to church every week but really struggled. I would get about halfway through mass and then I would break down in tears. Instead of being at church, I felt the need to be at the cemetery with Jenelle and Amy. I just wanted to feel closer to them than I did to God. I could get that feeling of closeness at the cemetery.

My cousin, David Stocker shared his thoughts about God and the Church.

He wrote:

Since the death of Jenelle, Amy and my Aunt Jean, I have thought a lot about God and the church. Of God, I come to only three choices:

The first choice is that there is no God. Of course, that means that there is no meaning to anything. We are all just random selections that happen to thrive under these atmospheric conditions. With no God, not only were Jenelle, Amy and my Aunt Jean's death meaningless but so also was the life they lived and the life we live as well.

The second choice is that there is a God but he is cruel and just toys with us like a cat playing with his prey. While explaining the death of Jenelle, Amy and Aunt Jean this choice just leads to hopelessness and despair in all things.

The third choice is there is a God who is good and loves. C.S. Lewis said it best in The Problem with Pain," The problem of reconciling human suffering with the existence of a God who loves, is only insoluble so long as we attach a trivial meaning to the word "love" and look on things as if man were the center of them. Man is not the center. God does not exist for the sake of man. Man does not exist for his own sake. "Thou hast created all things, and for thy pleasure they are and were created." We were made, not primarily that we may love God (though we were made for that too) but that God may love us, that we may become objects in which the divine love may rest "well pleased".

I do not understand the death of Jenelle, Amy, and Aunt Jean, I don't understand why the people, the pastor or the priest may have no words or the wrong words. I do not understand why I say the wrong words as well. The only good choice though is that God is good and loves. Randy and Char will be with Jenelle, Amy, and Aunt Jean again. All things will be made new again.

FORGIVENESS and FREE WILL

There comes a point when you need to make decisions about forgiveness. The anger I carried within me towards myself, my God, and the truck driver was eating me alive. I kept asking myself the following questions.

- Could I have done anything differently?
- Why did I make Amy go on that trip with Jenelle?
- Why didn't God protect my family?
- Did I forgive the truck driver for killing my family?
- Was Mom to blame?

Emotionally, I was a wreck for a long time. The above questions would bother me day and night. I could not sleep and was punishing myself.

I remember a time when I was at the cemetery, crying my heart out, when somebody placed their hands on my shoulders. It was a priest from Boise, Idaho. He was in town to give a presentation at a local Catholic Church. He asked me about what happened to Jenelle and Amy. I explained to him the circumstances of the accident and told him that I was struggling as to why God would not protect my family.

He explained to me that God gives everyone the free will to act on his or her own. Everything that we do on Earth affects the choices that we make. God provides humans the ability to make choices that are not determined by prior causes or by divine intervention. In other words, the truck driver that killed my family made the decision to drive a speeding truck and run a stop sign, while reading a book. It was his choice of stupidity, which killed my family. I must have needed that explanation, because shortly after that I was able to quit blaming God for the deaths. Instead, I started thanking him for the nine and nineteen years I had with Jenelle and Amy.

The question about me making Amy go on that trip haunted me for years. Every time that I questioned this decision, I came up with the same answer. It was the right thing to have her ride with Jenelle and spend time with Grandpa and Grandma Stocker.

I was able to forgive the truck driver. I realized that he did not intentionally kill my daughters. He made a terrible decision that resulted in their deaths. Although I forgave him, I still struggle to forgive his stupidity. When you hear stories about distracted driving, please keep our story in mind. The truck driver was reading while driving a fully loaded semi and speeding at the same time. He must live with the fact that he killed three people and nearly ruined the lives of hundreds more.

Was Mom to blame? This never crossed my mind. She loved Jenelle and Amy as much as anybody could love somebody else and would have done anything to protect them. I hate to say that I was glad that Mom died in the wreck but knowing that she is in heaven with Jenelle and Amy has brought a sense of peace to me throughout the years. Knowing that the three of them are in heaven together always makes me feel better.

How could our church have helped more?

Many of our close friends went to St. Peter's church with us. They were amazing people and helped us all of the time. We expected the same help from our church but we did not receive it. We were extremely disappointed with the lack of empathy and help from the church leadership. Maybe our expectations were too high. We expected to hear from the priest about our loss, maybe a card, a phone call, or a special prayer at church, but none of this happened. When we talked to Father about planning the funeral for Jenelle and Amy, he told us what to do and when to do it. I asked Father for a chance to address the congregation during the funeral, and he said no. Finally, after some persistence, he did agree to let me speak. We wanted to make the funeral service a "Celebration of Life" for Jenelle and Amy. In order to do that, we felt the need to share some stories about each girl. We also asked people that attended to share their stories as well. We still remember these amazing stories about our daughters and think that they substantially helped us in our grieving.

We concluded that some churches simply do not know how to help those with sudden loss. They are great at planning funeral dinners, visiting those in the hospital, and giving parishioners their last rites. We learned that in our case, the strength of our church was more in preparing people for death vs. helping those that are grieving because of death. If the person is still alive, the church can be very helpful. We felt neglected by the church.

Unfortunately, the loss of mom and the girls caused some of my family members to quit going to church. They could not get beyond the questions of "Why didn't God protect Mom and the girls?" "Why hasn't our church provided more support to us?"

My brother, Gary, scheduled an appointment with his parish priest several months after the accident. Gary said the meeting did not go well. While there was an element of sympathy and empathy expressed, the priest was clearly unskilled and uncomfortable dealing with sudden loss. The priest shared the sentiment "I am not very good at this (grief)." WOW! Not what you expect to hear from your local religious leader.

We all knew that God was with Mom, Jenelle, and Amy and that we would all see them again in heaven.

Chapter 24

Church Help
Planned vs. Unplanned death

Some congregations do an incredible job of responding to families at the time of a death. Church members bring food to the home and for the funeral meal. They support the families by attending the visitations and the funeral services. They send out sympathy cards offering thoughts and prayers. They visit the family in the days following the service. Beyond providing funerals, meals, and flowers—what else could or should a church do to support those that have suffered a significant loss? These are all great things, but personal contact and fellowship needs to be offered first.

Even at mass, the visitation and the funerals, people knew the girls had died, but chose not to approach us. I truly think they wanted to do something to extend support or comfort, but they did not know what to say or do. Therefore, they just stood there. At times, we even felt that we were providing comfort to those that should have been providing support and comfort to us. At the time of our loss, it was difficult for us to understand this reaction. Upon reflection, we now realize that people's lack of training, guidance, and experience was the main factor in their awkwardness around us. I think one of the main reasons I chose to write this book was to provide a resource to all who must confront this trauma in their lives.

Chapter 25

Does your Church have a
Bereavement Ministry?

Many churches do not have a plan on how to support those who have suffered a loss. Why, you ask? It is more a case of not understanding the different needs of grievers. I see multiple reasons why the bereaved and grieving easily drop off the church's radar.

Here are some we experienced.

- **Ministers or lay-people feeling awkward or uncomfortable**
Many people feel awkward and uncomfortable when trying to help or comfort grieving people. This goes for ministers and other religious leaders as well. When Mom and the girls died, our many friends and acquaintances wanted to do something but were not comfortable engaging us. They feared they would say the wrong thing or do something insensitive or that their efforts would cause further emotional distress. Grievers that suffer major loss rarely expect anyone to come up with the perfect thing to do or say. However, thoughts about "in a better place" and "God never gives you more than you can handle" were more hurtful than helpful to us and provided little comfort to our grief.

What was helpful were the friends who silently just sat with us. They did not feel compelled to say the right thing or fill the silence with words. They were just there for us. That meant the most to us. As my brother shared: "There are no words to describe what we went through."

- **Thoughts on our own mortality**

The second hindrance to ministering to the bereaved is the reluctance to focus on our own mortality. Acknowledging that our life in this world is finite can be uncomfortable. When dealing with traumatic loss, we cannot help but think about our own eventual death. It is much easier seeing my death as part of an earthly life and not as an end to my own existence. It is almost impossible not to think about your own life as you are trying to help others. Sometimes these thoughts get in the way and encourage us to keep our distance from those that are grieving. Do not let being anxious or fearful about your own mortality hurt your efforts to help the grieving. By admitting this up front, it might help you to provide more empathy for your congregation.

- **Unrealistic expectations about grief**

I am not sure what training a minister would have regarding comforting those who are grieving. If your training goes back to the five stages of grief written by Kubler-Ross, you need to understand that things have changed. Everybody grieves differently. There are no stages of grief; there is no defined period to grieve. There is nothing wrong with anger, crying, and depression. As a minister or even a lay-leader, I encourage you to get to know what everyone is going through and try to help him or her based on that knowledge.

The best expectation is not to have one. Allow the bereaved the freedom to navigate their own bereavement in their own ways and on their own timelines.

- **Follow-up Ideas for Ministers and/or Lay Ministers**

Remember how we all keep track of important dates in our lives. As a minister, I would encourage you to keep track of the important dates for members of your congregation who have suffered loss. It is so important that you are able to reach out to the family via the phone or better yet, in person, as fast as humanly possible. Please do not even consider sending a text or an email. People in this situation will be expecting your call and will most likely be disappointed if it does not come.

You do not need to say or do anything. Your presence and understanding will make an immediate difference and provide needed support. Remember, Hugs Help.

1. Within a few days of death, be sure to send a sympathy card, signed by the church staff and/or elders. Always add a personal note to your card. Let the griever know that you are praying for them and thinking about them. If possible, deliver the card in person.
2. Listen empathetically while encouraging them to share stories about their loved ones. Do not just hear what they are saying, try to understand what they are saying. Big difference.
3. Encourage them to cry—I always thought it was silly not to offer a Kleenex to somebody who was crying. Then I realized that this discouraged them from crying. Instead, reinforce their need to continue crying. Trust me. It is very therapeutic.
4. Provide a list of support groups available within the community. If possible, offer to attend one of them with your friend.
5. After two weeks, make a follow-up call to see how the person is doing. Do not ask what they need. Instead, be proactive and assume they need more support. Proactively send them some information on the type of death or share a book about grieving with them. Be sure to look for them at church. If they are a regular attendee that has missed a couple of weeks, he or she needs some extra help or attention.
6. On a regular basis, probably for the first year, take a few minutes to reach out to them either during church or during the week. Phone calls are OK, but personal visits mean so much more. If there are any bereavement meetings or gatherings at your church or within your community, personally invite them to attend.
7. On the anniversary of the death, send a letter acknowledging the occasion and offer ongoing support.

Key Points to Remember:

- Everyone grieves in his or her own way.
- The pain of a death diminishes by positive actions over time, but the sense of loss never completely disappears.
- Be careful with your use of Scripture. Not everybody is ready to talk about The Next Place, Heaven, or Hell. I read a story about a woman whose son went off to a Bible college. While there, he committed suicide. When she arrived for his memorial service, the president of the college told her that, since her son was a Christian, there was no reason to mourn because he was in heaven. For years, she bore the burden of not expressing her grief. Later, she met some friends that allowed her to tell her story. They encouraged her to grieve and cry; something she had not been able to do before. She knew that "heaven was a great place and believed in the resurrection, but her heart and soul still needed to process the loss of her son and the sudden departure from this world.

Ministering to those who grieve will be challenging, frustrating, and rewarding. You do not need an advanced degree in counseling or psychology to support those who are grieving. Sensitivity, patience, flexibility, and a follow-up plan are the basic requirements. By initiating a compassionate and timely follow-up, your ministry can help cure the broken-hearted.

As a church bereavement ministry, consider starting a database of people who have passed within the last two years. Include the following in your database:

- Name of deceased person
- Relationship of deceased person to church member
- Date of death
- Birthday of deceased person
- Address and phone member of church member
- Location of burial spot

Also, consider setting up some type of marketing effort within the church to help your members learn how to properly comfort or assist those that are going through the grieving process. Ideas include:

- Add monthly grief articles to your church bulletin
- Bring in guest speakers to discuss grieving and loss
- Add a section to the church library with books about grieving
- Promote your bereavement ministry to others in your community

Chapter 26

Religious and Cultural Observances of Death

The roles of religion and culture are very important for both victims and survivors because their answers to religious questions form their view of life, death and meaning. Many people do not know or understand their position on religion until disaster strikes. That is when they form their religious faith and beliefs.

Each culture has its own beliefs about the meaning and purpose of life and what happens after death. These rituals help people in those cultures better understand how to approach the death of a loved one. In some cultures, people may find death more bearable if they believe in life after death. Other cultures encourage people to believe that the spirit of someone who has died directly influences the living family members. They feel comforted by the belief that their loved one is watching over them.

Rituals offer people a way to process and express their grief. They also provide ways for the community to support the bereaved. A person who is bereaved is in a period of grief after a loss. Death can create a sense of chaos and disorder. Rituals and customs provide a sense of routine and normalcy as well as a set of directions that provide structure during the time surrounding death.

Rituals and customs can help address:

- How people care for each other as they approach death. This includes performing rituals both before and after death.
- How to handle a person's body after death. This includes how the person's body is cleansed and dressed, who handles the body, and whether to choose burial or cremation.
- Whether grief is expressed quietly and privately or loudly and publicly. This includes whether public crying or wailing is appropriate.
- Whether people of different genders or ages should grieve differently.
- What rituals people perform after death and who is included in these rituals.
- How long family members expect to grieve as well as how they dress and behave during the mourning period.
- How to honor the deceased over the lifetime of the family. This includes ongoing rituals to celebrate or talk with the deceased.
- What new roles family members expect to take on? This includes whether a widow remarries, or an oldest son becomes the family leader.

Most religions handle and talk about death in their own unique ways. It is important to understand how your grieving friend views death from a religious point of view. Below are some ways that different religions handle the loss of life.

Some churches:

- Pray the Sacraments of the Sick as the person is dying and involve confession and communion. If a person dies before the sacraments are given, the priest will anoint the deceased conditionally within three hours of the time of death. ·
- Use distinct phases to "The Mass of Christian Burial."
- Encourage prayers at the funeral home
- Welcome the body into the church
- Covering the casket with a white cloth
- Sprinkle the casket with holy water
- Say prayers after the Mass

- Escort the casket to the back of the church
- Bless the grave at the cemetery.
- Celebrate the one-month anniversary of death.

Other customs include:

- Encouraging treating the body with respect by discouraging autopsies and embalming.
- Teaching that viewing the corpse is disrespectful.
- Allowing funerals only on specific days of the week.
- Discouraging music and flowers while other customs encourage music and flowers.
- Asking family members and others to accompany the casket to the grave and to place a shovel of earth on the casket, as a sign of the finality of death.
- Discouraging visitors up to three days following the burial.
- Encouraging wearing a black pin with a torn ribbon, or a torn garment during the funeral and for the next week as a symbol of grief.
- Encouraging naming newborn babies after the deceased.
- Unveiling the tombstone at a special ceremony at the first anniversary of the death
- Keeping caskets open or closed, depending on the specific custom.
- Placing memorial items in the casket if the family approves.
- Accepting cremation
- Wearing black clothing as a part of mourning.
- Having memorial services instead of funerals and other immediate observances of death.
- Donating flowers and money are preferred ways to express condolences.
- Considering death as an act of God. Faithful followers believe that all the events during an individual's life, including the time and type of death, are predetermined by God.
- Encouraging people in grief to show their feelings openly by crying loudly. Some customs believe that crying cleans the soul.
- Staying with the family for up to seven days and never leaving them alone.

- Washing the body before the funeral ceremony begins. It is very upsetting to some cultures to bury a body without washing it first.

As you can see from above, various religions and cultural views about death and mourning are different. For your friend's sake, try to understand why they are grieving from a religious and cultural point of view.

Chapter 27

Grief and cultural sensitivity

There is no correct way to grieve. Mourning rituals that are normal to one culture may seem strange to another. It may be difficult to know how to be sensitive to a grieving person from a different cultural background. Consider the following questions as you seek to support a person with a different cultural background:

- What emotions and behaviors are normal grief responses within the person's own culture?
- What are the bereaved family's beliefs surrounding death?
- How many intimate experiences have they had with death?
- Who should attend mourning ceremonies?
- How are attendees expected to dress and act?
- Are gifts, flowers, or other offerings expected?
- What special days or dates will be significant for the bereaved family?
- What types of verbal or written condolence needs expressed?

Consider talking with someone who shares that cultural background or searching for information on the Internet to learn more about the customs and mourning practices of a person from another culture.

In each culture, **death is associated with rituals and customs** to help people with the grieving process. Rituals offer people ways to process and express their grief. They also provide ways for the community to support the bereaved. A person who is bereaved is in a period of grief and mourning after a loss. Some cultures **expect a dignified and quiet response to loss** while in other societies — mourners expect to be able to display their raw emotions. Emotions in grief, too, may vary between cultures. Some cultures expect feelings of loneliness or sadness while in other cultures, persons may respond with anger or rage.

Are death and our reactions to it that culturally different? If death is universal, should we not assume that grief should be as well? After all, since every culture experience death, should we not expect that every culture should grieve and mourn in similar ways? Cross-cultural studies on grief have taught us that the answer to that question is far more complex than we once believed. In fact, the only universal statement we can really affirm is that each culture has developed ways to respond to loss. Beyond that, there is little common ground. Each culture grieves losses differently. How and to whom we attach ourselves varies from one culture to another.

Chapter 28

My Thoughts on Distracted Driving
What is distracted driving?

The Webster dictionary tells us that, distracted means to be preoccupied, inattentive, unable to concentrate, or absent-minded. What it does not tell us is the cascading grief associated with distracted driving deaths is beyond human description. Therefore, the person that killed my family was driving while being preoccupied, inattentive, unable to concentrate, or absent-minded. Does this sound like you? Do you realize that in-attention at the wheel could lead to a loss similar to mine? Is it worth it trying to text and drive at the same time? Please keep this definition in mind when you are driving your car.

My brother, Gary, asked to add the following section to this book about distracted driving and how the death of mom, Jenelle, and Amy could have been prevented.

"As I write this – 18 years later – the tears still flow. No one should have to endure this, yet too many have, and too many more will get a similar phone call.

Randy and Char have shared their journey in the previous pages of this book. It was the cause of the crash that brought my fingers to my keyboard to focus on the real issue of July 22, 2003. A driver of a heavy truck made the conscious decision to drive a semi-truck while speeding and reading. He blew through a stop sign on a county road near Bloomington, IL and broadsided mom's car on the passenger side, where Jenelle and Amy were both sitting.

The legal process in Illinois (where the crash occurred) was cumbersome. With persistence, the county district attorney ultimately filed vehicular homicide charges against the driver of the semi-tractor truck that killed Mom, Jenelle, and Amy. The government did not prove these charges of reckless homicide during the August 2005 bench trial in Bloomington, IL.

The judge in the case stated that the driver was negligent, but that his actions were not criminal. A newspaper story the following day quoted Randy that he knew he would not be happy with any outcome. He did not want the driver to go to prison; he knew there was no intent to harm. However, he also did not want Mom, Jenelle, and Amy to have died in vain.

Randy met with the truck driver and his wife after the court hearing. He needed to hear some type of apology or explanation about what happened. The driver did apologize, but also admitted that he did not even get out of the truck to check on the girls. That really hurt my brother to know that the man that accidentally killed them, did not even bother to check on them.

This was not an accident. This was a singular crash caused by a driver whose distracted driving ended the lives of my mother, Jean, along with Jenelle and Amy.

Distracted driving has happened thousands of times since our tragedy. It will happen thousands of more times in the coming years. The reported statistics on the lives lost and damaged due to distracted drivers like the one that killed my family members are sobering. To a certain extent, we are all guilty of episodes of distracted driving. Given our family history, I am as focused of a driver as anyone. Yet, I know there are times I was lucky to avoid fender-bender type accidents or worse.

How many more times will this happen before our culture and our legal system develop sufficient consequences for distracted drivers. The truck driver probably had some significant legal expenses defending himself from the criminal charges brought by the state of Illinois. According to newspaper articles, the driver appeared to forlorn about the deaths he caused. However, as I write this, 18 years later, he has led a full life, watched his family grow, experienced holidays, and much more. My brother and our whole family have missed these things because of this distracted driver.

Apply these suggestions every time you drive:

- *When you drive, try to think of 'the phone call' – the one you could get if someone else is a distracted driver and their actions take your family members or friends.*
- *If you must reach for a drink, do it at a stop sign.*
- *Do not even think about reaching across a seat or down to the floor. If you must, in memory of all who have lost their lives to distracted drivers, please pull off the road. The risk of the consequences of not doing so are too immense to bear.*
- *When doing anything in your car that is not focused on driving, check all around you to make sure you are aware of your surroundings. There is an acronym we have in our family. It is LSA. It means 'Lacking Situational Awareness'. Too many times our hectic lives force us to react and not anticipate. The driver of the truck that killed my mother, Jenelle, and Amy clearly lacked it.*
- *Educate your children and new drivers in your family on the potential consequences of distracted driving. Go ahead and share Randy's story with them. Make sure they realize that if they lack situational awareness while driving, they could end somebody's life or maybe their own.*

We all think these types of accidents can only happen to the "other guy or the other driver". That is not true. Please take every preventative action that you can while driving so you are not the cause of an accident like the one that killed Mom, Jenelle, and Amy.

Chapter 29

Do hugs really help?

I chose **HUGS HELP** as the title of my book because most, but not all, people want or need an embrace or a hug. To a griever, a hug is sort of like "sharing the pain with somebody else for a few seconds". That few seconds or minutes of sharing the pain—is very therapeutic.

I had just spent a few days with my 86-year-old father, Frank. As I was leaving his home in Gibson City, he gave me a hug. While driving back home to Rochester, Minnesota, I was trying to think of a name for this book. I wanted the reader to be able to understand that being able to both give and receive hugs after our tragic loss helped us to get through our tremendous battles with grief and depression. So, yes, in our case, Hugs Helped.

I did some research on the benefits of hugging and learned that our bodies contain cuddle nerves—I had never heard this term before. It refers to a special network of nerves that stimulate a pleasurable response to stroking. The next time you are giving somebody a hug, ask them, "How are your cuddle nerves feeling?"

In answer to the question, "Do Hugs Help?" the correct answer is yes. Below are some of the proven benefits of hugs.

- **Hugs reduce stress.** We were so "stressed out" after the accident. Not only did we appreciate hugs, but we also needed them. To us, hugs were like sharing our pain with another person. In addition, we had lots of pain for a long time. Research has found that embracing or hugging reduces the amount of stress hormones in our bodies. This helps to release tension and sends calming messages to our brains. Have you ever hugged a friend or family member after a long day and thought to yourself, "Wow, I really needed that!"

- **Hugging is heart healthy.** There is a hormone called oxytocin in our bodies. Embracing activates this hormone and makes us feel warm and fuzzy. Studies show that receiving a hug prior to a stressful situation can help reduce both blood pressure and heart rate while helping to heal negative feelings such as loneliness, isolation, anger, and grief.
- **Hugging can reduce the fear of mortality.** There was study done that showed hugging an inanimate object, like a teddy bear or a blanket, helps to reduce the anxiety towards death. A hug may make an individual feel happy by reducing feelings of loneliness and the harmful physical effects of stress. Hugs can change negative moods by helping the brain and body generate these feel-good hormones.

Last, and most importantly, hugs just make you feel good. In other words—

HUGS HELP

Thank you for reading my book. If this book helped you in any way, please consider sharing it with a friend. To follow our blog, go to www.hugshelp. org and click on "Join our Hugs Help Facebook group".

Ten ways to help those who are grieving

1. Fully understand the grieving process:
   - Everybody grieves differently
   - Most people are uncomfortable around the grieving
   - Grief is a long-term process
   - Anything can trigger a reaction to grief
2. Make regular contact and/or visits:
   - Stay in touch for several months or longer.
   - Grievers never forget their loved ones. You shouldn't either.

3. Be Proactive
   - Do not ask the griever to call you if they need something. Odds are that they will never call. Instead, be proactive and do something to help-ANYTHING.
4. Do not overpromise
   - People who have lost a loved one have already suffered the "ultimate disappointment". Do not hurt them again by making promises you can't keep.
5. Proactively talk about the deceased person
   - Tell stories
   - Share pictures
   - Share memories-good or bad
6. Never offer advice—only offer options.
   - Encourage the griever to make their own decisions.
   - Don't tell them what you think they should do. Instead, give the options or ideas
7. Grief makes people fragile.
   - Treat them with extra care and attention
   - Show empathy
   - Be patient
   - Provide lots of hugs and support
8. Be smart in what you say
   - Our society places too much emphasis on "getting on with your life".
   - Think before you speak. The wrong words will cause pain for a griever.
   - Encourage your friends to cry and grieve vs. repressing their grief
9. Remember special days
   - A simply "thinking of you" phone call means so much to someone in pain.
   - Stay away from texts and emails. Pick up the telephone and speak to the person you care about.
10. Be patient
    - Grief can be long term.
    - Never rush a grieving person to make a decision or change.

Questions to ask yourself prior to trying to comfort your grieving friend

- What does this loss mean to this person at this time?
- How does what I say or do affect my friend the griever?
- What type of support does my friend need?
- If I were in this situation, how would I feel and what would mean the most to me?
- Am I someone my friend can confide in and trust with his/her most personal thoughts and feelings?
- Am I someone who is not judgmental and allows my grieving friend to say what he/she needs to say when they need to say it?
- Am I someone who is there when others "walk away?"

Acknowledgements

It was very hard to write this book. Re-reading the many great stories about Mom, Jenelle, and Amy, brought me to tears on numerous occasions. Researching the accident again so I had the details correct brought back so many terrible memories from that July day in 2003.

First of all, I want to thank my beautiful wife, Char. She provided excellent content and stories that are a big part of the book. She was also there when she found me crying in my office after writing a section about Jenelle or Amy. A good friend shared with us that a very high percentage of marriages fail after losing a child. Although we struggled on occasion, we were determined to not lose both our daughters and our marriage. We will be celebrating our 40th Wedding Anniversary in June 2022. So, we beat the odds. Char was always there with a big hug. We all know that HUGS HELP!

My son, Matt, and daughter, Melissa, were both strong supporters of the book. They realized how important it was for me to share my story about grief and grieving. They both provided feedback as well as constructive criticism. I appreciate your help and your support these past six months. I love you both, lots.

My brother, Gary, kept me on track the entire writing and marketing process. We had weekly strategy sessions throughout the writing of the book. He is my technical advisor and has taught me so much about how to promote and market my book. He also shared some great stories from his own experiences. Thank you, Big Brother. I couldn't have done it without your help. Special thanks to my father, Frank Stocker. You were amazing when I needed you the most. Thanks for letting me "cry on your shoulder". You are an amazing father and I love you lots.

Finally, I need to thank my mother, Jean, and my daughters, Jenelle, and Amy. Although they are no longer with us, they continued to inspire me from heaven. Whenever I get down or depressed, they sent me a sign saying that I need to continue with my work because it will help many others who are grieving. All three of them were amazing people that cared for others and always tried to help in any way they could. Thank you for your "heavenly inspiration". I miss you and love you lots. Dad

There were so many more people that helped me with this book. If I mentioned all of you, my book would be double in size. You know who you are and that your help was greatly appreciated.